*COLUMBIA STUDIES
IN ECONOMICS*

7

International Trade and Development Theory

INTERNATIONAL TRADE
and
DEVELOPMENT THEORY

Ronald Findlay

COLUMBIA UNIVERSITY PRESS
New York and London   1973

Library of Congress Cataloging in Publication Data

Findlay, Ronald.
    International trade and development theory. *see slip*
    (Columbia studies in economics, 7)
    Bibliography: p. 221 - 226.
    1. Economic development—Mathematical models.
    2. Commerce—Mathematical models. I. Title.
    II. Series.
    HD82.F46   382   73–8623
    ISBN 0–231–03546–2

To
K. C. H.

Preface

THIS BOOK originated in a chapter of a doctoral dissertation submitted at the Massachusetts Institute of Technology in 1960. For inspiration and instruction in the art of economic theorizing, I am indebted to my mentor since my undergraduate days, Dr. Tun Thin, Professors Evsey Domar, Charles Kindleberger, Paul Samuelson, and Robert Solow and to my friend and fellow graduate student of the late 1950s, Dr. Harry Grubert. Further ideas were developed at Rangoon University and the Institute of Economics, Rangoon, where discussions with R.M. Sundrum and Dr. Aye Hlaing were most helpful. The bulk of the thinking and writing, however, was done in the last four years at Columbia University. I would like to thank Harry Johnson and Peter Kenen for bringing me to a most hospitable and stimulating environment. My work has benefited from the comments and suggestions of many colleagues, in particular from those of Raymond Lubitz and Stanislaw Wellisz, and from the interest and encouragement of my friends Carlos Diaz Alejandro and Jagdish Bhagwati. My greatest debt is to my student Dewey Seeto whose alert reading of the drafts of various chapters has saved me from many mistakes and careless formulations. His extensions of some of my results as part of his own doctoral dissertation have also been very encouraging. I hope that none of these good people will be embarrassed unduly by my associating them with this work. I wish to give them the usual ritual absolution of all responsibility for its many shortcomings.

This book was essentially completed while I enjoyed a Ford Foundation Faculty Research Fellowship for 1971–72. It began while I was a graduate student at M.I.T., also on a Ford Foundation fellowship. In the jargon of economic theory, I do not know what the "objective function" of this organization is, but I am deeply grateful for twice being its beneficiary.

Chapters 2, 3, 7, 9, and 10 are slightly revised versions of papers published in the *Economic Journal*, *Review of Economic Studies*, *Journal of Political Economy*, *Journal of International Economics*, and *Trade, Balance of Payments and Growth* (Papers in International Economics in Honor of Charles P. Kindleberger) edited by J. Bhagwati, R. W. Jones, R.A. Mundell, and J. Vanek (North Holland: Amsterdam, 1971). I am grateful to the editors of these journals and to the editor of the volume in honor of my teacher for permission to reprint these selections. The titles and dates of the papers are listed under my name in the bibliography. In revising Findlay (1966) for Chapter 2, I have taken into account an algebraic slip pointed out by Mabro (1968).

Contents

PART FOUR: STRUCTURAL DISEQUILIBRIUM

International Trade and Development Theory

CHAPTER 1

Introduction

THIS INTRODUCTORY chapter provides some background and perspective on the nature of the problems to be dealt with by means of a highly selective survey of the related literature, followed by a brief outline of the contents of the rest of the book.

I

Since the very beginnings of the emergence of economics as a scientific discipline, its practitioners have maintained that there is a crucial link between the nature and extent of a country's foreign trade and the rate and pattern of its general economic development. The Mercantilist obsession with trade surpluses, for example, can partly be interpreted as a recognition of the need for some source of an expansion of liquidity to lower interest rates and stimulate investment at a time when appropriate financial institutions had not yet evolved. The Marxian emphasis on "primitive accumulation" could also perhaps be accounted for in the same terms. Adam Smith clearly envisioned a process in which foreign trade played a vital part in extending the market and hence leading to increases in productivity through the scope given for greater specialization. Ricardo stressed the relationships between trade, income distribution, and savings in his advocacy of the repeal of the Corn Laws. John Stuart Mill pointed out the importance of trade as a source for the spread of technology and the creation of wants that provide the incentive for greater effort on the part of the populations of traditional economies. Marshall, in a famous quote, said "the causes which determine the economic progress of nations belong to the study of international trade."[1]

In spite of all this, however, the pure theory of international trade as fashioned in the tradition of Ricardo, Mill, Marshall—and down to the early 1950s in the works of Samuelson, Meade, and other well-known economists—has concerned itself almost exclusively with the patterns of production, consumption, distribution, and exchange which emerge as a result of trade between economies with given tastes, technology, and resource endowment. The only attention specifically directed toward developmental problems within the standard theory was in the narrowly restricted domain of arguments for "infant industry" tariff protection.

The mainstream of trade theory has neglected development, and similarly many of the major contributions to the theory of economic development that has been emerging in the last few decades have neglected to consider international trade as an integral part of their approach. This is true of Rosenstein-Rodan's (1943) famous article for example, and also of the very influential *Problems of Capital Formation in Underdeveloped Countries* by Ragnar Nurkse (1953) and *Strategy of Economic Development* by Albert Hirschmann (1958). On the other hand, prominent writers such as Myrdal have considered trade relations between the "center" and the "periphery" as a crucial aspect of the problem of the relative underdevelopment of the latter and Nurkse (1959) himself examined the trade-development nexus explicitly in his Wicksell Lectures.

Myrdal (1956, 1957) in particular has concentrated on the ways in which development at the center tends to be at the expense of development in the periphery. While admitting, of course, that there are favorable "spread" effects such as the growth of markets, the availability of complex new products, and the creation of new technology that result from rising income levels in the center, Myrdal has stressed the negative "backwash" effects that operate

[1]Marshall (1920) p. 270.

to the detriment of the periphery, such as the diversion of capital and skilled labor in the so-called "brain drain." These problems are familiar to students of regional inequality within nations, and the observation has often been made that the underdevelopment of the Third World is an Appalachian or Mezzogiorno problem on a global scale. If the analogy is accepted, then an important recent piece of empirical research on intranational regional inequality would appear to hold out considerable hope for those worried about the "widening gap" between the advanced and backward parts of the globe. On the basis of both cross-section and time-series data from the United States and other countries, J. Williamson (1965) has found that regional inequality is an inverted U-shaped function of the national level of per capita income, with the "backwash" effects apparently dominating at first but with the "spread" effects coming to the fore later on.

Although he has expressed himself on many aspects of the trade and development connection, the idea most commonly associated with Raul Prebisch is that there is a secular tendency for the terms of trade to turn against the less developed countries because of certain technical and institutional features associated with the demand and supply for primary commodities and manufactures. Speculation about secular tendencies of the terms of trade between agricultural and industrial products has a long and interesting history, going back at least to Torrens, who held that they would move in favor of agriculture and against industry, on the grounds that the former was characterized by decreasing and the latter by increasing returns. Keynes and D. H. Robertson also held this view, and writing in 1915 Robertson even went so far as to say that the tendency for the terms of trade to turn against manufactures was "perhaps the most significant economic fact in the world today."[2] In his 1938 article on the "Future of International Trade," where he introduced the famous phrase about trade being an "engine of growth," Robertson said that manufacturing technology could eventually be diffused fairly evenly throughout the world whereas the distribution of natural resources is skewed and

[2]Robertson (1915) p. 169.

continuing economic development would tend to turn the terms of trade in favor of the owners of these scarce gifts of nature.[3]

In a 1950 United Nations document on *The Economic Development of Latin America and its Principal Problems* Prebisch put forward several reasons why it could be expected that the secular tendency for the terms of trade would be the opposite of that envisaged in the tradition of Torrens, Keynes, and Robertson. The main points were that the income elasticity of demand for manufactures was greater than unity while it was less than unity for food, that the nature of technical progress in advanced countries was such as to develop synthetic substitutes for natural raw materials, and that manufactures were produced under monopolistic conditions while primary products had highly competitive markets. Empirical verification was claimed to be found in a U.N. study which drew on some work by W. Schlote on Britain's terms of trade from 1870. Haberler (1961) and other writers have questioned the theoretical reasoning underlying the Prebisch thesis and later studies by Kindleberger (1956) on Europe and Robert Lipsey (1963) on the United States reveal no clear secular tendency one way or the other for the terms of trade.

The theoretical core of Ragnar Nurkse's 1953 book was his concept of the "vicious circle" of poverty linking low per capita incomes with inability to save and a low inducement to invest, which was to be broken by his strategy of "balanced growth" on a broad front. As it stood, this thesis could have been attacked on the ground that it neglected possibilities of unbalanced growth through international specialization. Nurkse's 1959 Wicksell Lectures, however, can be interpreted as an answer to this criticism. Here he asserted that while in the nineteenth century, trade had indeed been an "engine of growth," it had ceased to be so in the twentieth, except for the oil exporters. Low income-elasticities, synthetic substitutes, and the differences between the United States (with its extensive natural-resource base) and Britain as the dominant "center" country were given as the cause for the slow

---

[3]For an interesting review of this literature, see chapter 8 of Rostow (1952), "The Terms of Trade in Theory."

growth of demand for primary goods. Prospects for manufactured exports from the less developed countries were also not held to be good. This left expansion for the home market as the only alternative, so that the "balanced growth" strategy turns out to be appropriate after all. A recent article by Irving Kravis (1970) has seriously questioned the validity of the Nurkse thesis for the nineteenth century and asserts that trade was more a "handmaiden" than an "engine" of growth for the most successful developers in that period. The success of trade-based expansion in for example Hong Kong, Taiwan, and Korea in recent years also throws some doubt on the sharp contrast that Nurkse drew between nineteenth- and twentieth-century trade patterns.

The literature that has so far been mentioned, while rich in perceptive insights and what might be called "stylized history," has nevertheless been deficient because of its lack of any explicitly theoretical foundation. The next section will briefly examine more formal analytical models of trade and growth.

II

In spite of its traditionally static character, the standard, two-factor, two-good, two-country model of pure trade theory is able to say something useful about the effects of capital accumulation, population growth, and technical change on the volume and terms of trade. The comparative-statics methods of general equilibrium theory can readily be applied to once-over changes in the given endowment of "capital" or labor or in the given production functions for the goods. The late 1950s saw many contributions along these lines following the lead of Harry Johnson (1955), who was himself inspired by Sir John Hicks's (1953) famous Inaugural Lecture on the long-run dollar problem. T. M. Rybczynski (1955) proved an indispensable theorem on the effects of a change in factor endowment on output levels of the two goods at fixed relative product prices and the effects of neutral and biased changes in technology were worked out by Findlay and Grubert (1959). Various outcomes are possible for the terms of trade, depending upon which factor expands, which sector experiences the technical progress, the extent to which the progress is neutral or biased in favor of labor or capital, the relative factor-intensities of the two goods and the pattern of home and foreign demand. An exhaustive taxonomy is provided in a survey article by Johnson (1959) and Ronald Jones (1965) has achieved an elegant mathematical synthesis of all these results, drawing on the work of Amano (1964) and Takayama (1964).

One of the striking results obtained in this context was Jagdish Bhagwati's (1958) demonstration of conditions under which exogenous growth, due to factor expansion or technical change, would be "immiserizing" in the sense that the loss of welfare due to deterioration of the terms of trade would outweigh the gain from the larger volume of production. Edgeworth (1894), who was aware of this possibility, referred to it as "damnifying." The possibility arises intuitively when, at constant relative product prices, the supply of the exportable commodity expands by a greater amount than domestic demand for it, so that the surplus has to be dumped abroad, the resultant decline in the terms of trade being the greater the lower the price-elasticity of demand in the foreign country. For sufficiently high values of the "output-elasticity of supply,"[4] and low values of domestic income-elasticity and foreign price-elasticity of demand, the deterioration of the terms of trade can be so great as to more than offset the rise in real income at constant relative prices due to the expansion. It is clear that this situation can only arise under laissez-faire, since a government intervention could always at worst leave trade unchanged, while consuming the additional output made possible by the expansion.

These results have an obvious bearing on the broader issues of trade and development discussed in the first section; they were briefly touched on by Nurkse in an appendix to the Wicksell Lectures, the last work before his untimely death. Somewhat surprisingly, he seems to have been very suspicious of the logic and em-

---

[4]This is defined as the proportionate change in the output of a commodity divided by the proportionate change in the total value of production at constant relative product prices.

pirical relevance of the Johnson-Bhagwati approach, particularly the concept of output-elasticity of supply, the nature of which he apparently misunderstood. He asks, "But what is it that is supposed to produce the immiserizing growth? Obviously not the price system; if the terms of trade are falling why should additional resources crowd into the export sector? Immiserizing growth seems to rest on the novel concept of 'output elasticity of supply,' which does not operate through relative price changes but assumes instead something like a fixed propensity of factor increments to go into certain predetermined lines of activity."[5]

It is clear from this passage that Nurkse did not have a grasp of the Rybczynski theorem on which the Bhagwati point rests. The theorem assumes that there are two factors (say land and labor), and two goods, one of which could be thought of as a primary exportable and the other as a manufactured good. The former is land-intensive and the latter labor-intensive in the Lerner-Samuelson sense (that at any factor-price ratio the land-labor ratio in the primary good would be higher than in manufactures). Constant returns to scale are assumed for both production functions.

Suppose that there is an exogenous increase in the supply of land. To determine its effects on the pattern of production and the terms of trade, assume first that relative product prices, and hence relative factor prices, are held constant. The land-labor ratios in each sector will then be unchanged, so that the only way in which the additional land can be absorbed is for the output of the primary commodity, which is relatively land-intensive, to increase. But since input coefficients do not change, labor must be drawn away from manufactures, the output of which therefore has to contract absolutely. Thus not only the additional land but some land and labor previously allocated to manufactures goes to increase the output of the primary exportable. If domestic demand for this good rises at constant prices by less than the increase in production, there will be an excess supply of the primary exportable and a corresponding excess demand for the manufactured importable, which turns the terms of trade against the country.

[5]Nurkse (1959) p. 58.

This change in the terms of trade will reduce output and the land and labor used in the primary sector as compared with the hypothetical constant relative price situation.

It can thus be seen that Nurkse's comment confuses cause and effect. Additional resources do not perversely crowd into the export sector in spite of the falling terms of trade. It is the "crowding" to accommodate the factor expansion that creates the fall in the terms of trade which alleviates the crowding. It is precisely the free play of the price system that brings about the result. What Nurkse must have intuitively felt, although he did not express it explicitly, was that a rational policy of state intervention could always overcompensate the "immiserization" effect, which is certainly true.[6]

The same model that is used in this literature on the comparative statics of trade theory has also been the basis of the extensive contributions on the two-sector growth model of closed economies, in which the two goods are specified as a capital and a consumption good respectively, and the mode of analysis is explicitly dynamic with labor growing exogenously at a fixed rate but with the system itself determining the rate of growth of capital by a savings function of some kind or other. The growth and trade strands of the neoclassical two-sector model were linked in a paper of remarkable technical ingenuity by Oniki and Uzawa (1965). This paper itself, and the subsequent contributions stemming from it, however, have all been concerned with formal problems of the existence and stability of the solution to the system of differential equations involved, and the relevance to developmental problems is certainly not apparent.

III

Most contributions to the theory of economic development have postulated the existence of "disguised unemployment" or "surplus labor" on an extensive scale in the typical underdeveloped

---

[6]Nurkse's error is quoted approvingly by Meier (1968) p. 52 in his otherwise useful survey of trade and development issues.

economy. It might even be said that "surplus labor" in some form or other is what provides the crucial structural difference between underdeveloped and advanced economies. Such characteristics as a low level of per capita income or a high proportion of the labor force in agriculture cannot in themselves serve as analytical bases for demarcation, however useful they may be for purposes of practical classification, since one is hard put to define any particular level of these variables as a "threshold" across which there is a "transformation of quantity into quality," as the Marxists put it. Attempts to base the distinction in terms of the rate of growth rather than the level of income cannot do the job either, since there is no clear relation between the extent of underdevelopment and rate of growth.

The *locus classicus* of the "surplus labor" hypothesis—and of the model of development based upon it—is of course the celebrated article of W. Arthur Lewis (1954). Other writers, notably Rosenstein-Rodan and Nurkse, had previously advanced the concept of "disguised unemployment," but the achievement of the Lewis paper was in embedding this concept in the framework of a model of a "dual economy" in which there is an advanced or "modern" sector and a backward or "traditional" sector from which "unlimited supplies" of labor can be drawn at a fixed wage rate for employment in the former sector. The employment level in the modern sector is determined by the capital stock in that sector on the hypothesis that profits are maximized, so that the marginal product of labor is equated to the fixed wage rate determined exogenously by conditions in the traditional sector plus whatever margin is necessary to induce labor to move. The accumulation of capital is governed—as in Marx, Ricardo, and the modern Cambridge growth theory—by the propensity to save out of profits. Development is envisioned as a process whereby the modern sector expands relative to the traditional sector until a point is reached at which further employment in the modern sector begins to pull up the wage rate and the model no longer applies. Orthodox economic theory presumably takes over at this point.

In its basic structure the Lewis model does not need any particular specification for conditions in the traditional sector, which can be treated simply as a "black box" from which labor can be drawn at a fixed wage. Oddly enough, however, some of his asides about the utilization of labor in agriculture have attracted more comment and controversy than the essential characteristics of the model, which focuses on the expansion of the modern sector. In particular the proposition that the marginal product of labor is zero in agriculture has somehow been regarded as a crucial assumption of the Lewis model, and several writers have devoted much attention to attacking it on both theoretical and empirical grounds. Unfortunately, much of this criticism assumes that by marginal product of labor is meant the marginal product of additional man-hours and not the marginal product of an additional worker. The situation Lewis envisions is one in which the number of man-hours that the agricultural labor force can gainfully spend is limited by shortage of land and equipment, so that withdrawal of part of them for employment in the modern sector will increase the amount of work done by those remaining so that output remains the same as before. This kind of underemployment, not only in agriculture but in urban petty trades and services as well, provides the reservoir which together with natural increase and possibly foreign immigration enables the modern sector to increase employment at a fixed wage rate at whatever pace is permitted by saving out of profits. The ability to expand employment at a rate faster than the natural increase of labor at more or less fixed wage rates for some length of time is the key hypothesis of the dual economy model and, as Lewis says, it is "inconsistent neither with history nor with reason."[7]

However, it is of course possible to go beyond the original basic model and provide an endogenous explanation of the wage level, say in terms of the average product of labor in agriculture. A number of writers attempt to do this, notably Fei and Ranis (1964), Jorgenson (1961), Sen (1966), and Wellisz (1968) in all of which further institutional detail is introduced regarding land owner-

---

[7]Lewis (1968) p. 4.

ship and tenure, income sharing within the family, and relations between migrating workers and members of their families remaining on the farm.

An alternative avenue of further amplification and articulation of the underlying logic of the Lewis model is provided by the different specifications that can be adopted for the structure of production and exchange within the "modern" sector itself, which Lewis himself leaves open. His procedure has the advantage of generality, in that a wide variety of cases can be accommodated within the same framework. On the other hand detailed and specific results about a number of interesting features of the developmental process can only be obtained if distinct, although possibly overlapping, cases are identified.

The simplest assumption to make is that the output of the modern sector is a homogeneous universal commodity that is both the only wage good and the only capital good. In this case the modern sector is completely self-contained and there is no trade with either the traditional sector or the outside world. The model becomes just like the one-sector neoclassical growth model of Solow (1956) and Swan (1956), with the exception that the wage rate is a parameter and the growth rate of employment a variable instead of the other way around. Nothing of very much interest emerges from this specification. With the wage rate given, profit maximization equates the marginal product of labor to this parameter and the corresponding marginal product of capital is the rate of profit, which determines the balanced rate of growth of employment, capital, and output in conjunction with the propensity to save out of profits, all of wages being consumed. The objective function can however be changed from simple profit maximization in each period to maximization of the integral of utility from consumption over a finite or infinite horizon, in the manner of the classic article by Ramsey (1928). Papers by Marglin (1967) and Dixit (1968) have explored this problem: Dixit, in particular, with great refinement and technical skill. The marginal product of labor is required to be below the given wage rate for the initial phase of the optimal consumption program, so that employment and consumption are both greater at any given level of the capital stock than under the objective of profit maximization at each moment.

If the modern sector is regarded as urban industry, the problem of food supply for the labor force in this sector immediately arises, and some form of trade—with either the traditional sector or the outside world—has to be introduced into the model and with it the need for an analysis of what determines the terms and the volume of trade. Trade with the rest of the world could be taken as sufficiently negligible as to be safely neglected, as in some cases of great historical interest such as the Soviet Union in the 1920s and 1930s, or the People's Republic of China after the break with the Soviet Union. The Soviet experience of the 1920s is particularly fascinating both in the nature of the actual problems that were encountered, such as the famous "scissor's crisis," and in the theoretical debates to which they gave rise among such figures as Bukharin and Preobrazhensky. These debates have been examined vividly and with great insight by Alexander Erlich (1960).

Chapters 2 and 3 of this book will be concerned with analyzing alternative development strategies within the context of a closed dual economy in which the modern sector is operated on the basis of state ownership and central planning and the peasant sector consists of independent owner-cultivators. The model thus does not apply to the postcollectivization situation in the Soviet Union, for example, in which the control of the planners extended over the entire economy. The output of the industrial sector is divided between consumer and capital goods, the former of which also serves as an input into the system in the sense that production of it is required to obtain labor from the traditional sector with which it can be exchanged for food. The objective function of the planners is taken as either the maximization of the growth rate or of the level of consumption or capital goods output at some specified horizon. The allocation of investment between the consumption and capital goods sectors of a planned economy is also the subject of a model originally put forward by the Soviet economist Feldman, which became widely known only after it was elaborated and refined by Domar (1957) and independently rediscovered by the statistician P. C. Mahalanobis (1953), who was for some years the chief architect of Indian planning. The properties of this model will be contrasted with our variant of the Lewis model.

The second part of the book, chapters 4-6, will introduce international trade into the dual-economy model in three alternative ways. In chapter 4 the modern sector is able to exercise monopoly power over the traditional sector in exchanging manufactured consumer goods for food, which can also be obtained at fixed terms of trade from the rest of the world. The relation of the optimal internal terms of trade to the given external terms will be explored on the hypothesis that the growth rate of the modern sector is to be maximized.

In chapter 5 the modern sector is first conceived as being a pure "enclave" or plantation economy in which there is complete specialization on a primary exportable, with capital goods and manufactured consumer goods both being imported. The rate of growth is shown to be determined by the rate at which the world demand curve for the primary good shifts over time for any given price. This specification enables formal analytical treatment of the consequences of the general contention by Nurkse, Prebisch, and others that the growth of developing countries is inhibited by the sluggishness of world demand for primary exports. The possibility of producing manufactured consumer goods is then introduced and the question of whether this enables the economy to escape from externally imposed limitations on its growth rate through import substitution and manufactured exports is examined.

Chapter 6 presents a growth model of an open dual economy with a rather complex "two-level" production structure in which labor and capital make both a nontradable or domestic good and "foreign exchange," both of which are used in turn to make consumption and capital goods. This model incorporates foreign trade and the shadow price of foreign exchange into the planning model discussed in Part One.

Taken together the five chapters of Parts One and Two constitute a set of "variations on a theme by Lewis" that are intended to extend his original vision of the development process by specify-

ing a number of alternative structural patterns for his generic
"modern sector," each of which is an idealization of some particular type of developing economy. The two chapters of Part One are
concerned with large and relatively closed economies making
their own capital goods. Some aspects of development strategy in
Soviet Russia in the 1920s or in China and India today can
perhaps be illuminated by this approach. Chapter 5 goes to the
polar case of a primary exporting economy that has no capital
goods sector of its own and that is totally dependent on earnings
from its primary exports and success in import substitution and
perhaps eventual export of manufactured consumer goods to obtain its capital-good requirements. Countries such as Ghana,
Malaysia, Ceylon, and smaller Latin American economies come to
mind in this connection. Chapter 6 discusses an economy that has
a domestic capital goods sector but that requires foreign exchange
for its functioning, and is therefore an intermediate case in comparison with the two earlier ones.

In all the cases development occurs when the "modern sector"
converts its profits into capital accumulation and employment
increases at a fixed wage. This is the basic Lewis theme. The
"variations" that are provided here are the result of different possible answers to questions about the sources, whether internal or
external, of the profits and of the capital goods into which they are
transformed. Lewis himself, in his theoretical exploration of trade
problems, gives up his own model and goes back to the primitive
Ricardo model, which he uses with breathtaking imagination and
skill, as in his analysis of the terms of trade between temperate
and tropical countries in his recent Wicksell Lectures (1969).
Most of the other writers on the dual-economy model also concen-
trate on the closed version. Fei and Ranis, for example, do not introduce trade until the last chapter of their book. The studies of
Part Two may therefore be of some use in linking trade theory to
the dual-economy model.

Part Three, consisting of chapters 7 to 9, is concerned with the
concept of comparative advantage in growing economies not characterized by the dualism hypothesis. Chapter 7 distinguishes between instantaneous and long-run comparative advantage. The

former is determined by whatever factor proportions prevail at the moment and the latter by those which will ultimately prevail as a consequence of growth with a fixed savings ratio and labor growth rate. Chapter 8 explores the consequences of the inability to shift capital stock between sectors once it has been installed. It is shown that this could lead under some conditions to the optimal allocation of investment being such that the current return on investment is not equalized between sectors even though it is possible to do so. This raises some difficult problems about foresight in a decentralized competitive system—problems that do not exist in the usual malleable capital model. In chapter 9 the question of whether it is possible to rank the sectors of a protected economy in order of comparative advantage by the use of such criteria as the domestic resource cost of foreign exchange (as suggested by Michael Bruno (1963, 1967) and Anne Krueger (1966), or the required rate of effective protection (as advocated by Bela Balassa and Daniel Schydlowsky) (1968) is examined.

Part Four discusses some influential ideas about the persistence of "structural" disequilibrium in developing economies as a result of inflexibility in the allocation of resources in response to changes in relative prices. Chapter 10 deals with the "two gap" theory, associated with the name of Hollis Chenery, and introduces the effect of relative price variations into the macro model that is usually used in this context. Chapter 11 attempts to formulate more precisely some contentions of the Latin American "structuralist" school regarding inflation, devaluation, and stabilization.

Part One

THE CLOSED DUAL ECONOMY
*Capital Accumulation
and "Productive Consumption"*

CHAPTER 2

Optimal Investment Allocation between Consumer Goods and Capital Goods

CHAPTERS 2 and 3 are both concerned with the analysis of a situation in which the modern sector of the dual economy has a capital goods and a consumer goods branch and in which foreign trade is excluded. This last assumption needs justification, particularly in a book entitled *International Trade and Development Theory*. Three reasons can be offered. First, there are some instances in which the underdeveloped economy is sufficiently large and diversified for foreign trade to be a small fraction of its GNP, say five percent or less. This may be reinforced by political circumstances, as in the isolation of the Soviet Union in the 1920s and 1930s and China in the 1960s. India and Brazil, while obviously still dependent on trade for complex and sophisticated products, are nevertheless now becoming increasingly able to meet their own capital-goods requirements. Second, frustration with difficulties in international trade and suspicions of neocolonialism have made many people advocate a path of autonomous or "inward looking" development even for countries that would normally be export oriented. Third, for analytical purposes it is convenient to have a closed-economy reference point for comparison with the models of development with trade that will be examined in the other chapters of the book.

The first section of this chapter presents a brief survey of the nature of the problem to be examined and the related literature that will be relevant for this chapter and the next.

I

The pattern of planned industrialization exemplified by the earlier phases of Soviet history is for the state to collectivize the peasantry to ensure sufficient deliveries of food to the urban areas, and, within industry itself, for a high proportion of available resources to be devoted to the capital goods producing department, leaving the production of consumer goods in comparative neglect.

This procedure of emphasizing capital goods production relatively early in the stage of industrialization has seemed to many Western observers to be putting the cart before the horse if compared with the "textiles first" path of development suggested by the experience of their own countries. The difference is no doubt partly due to the great changes that have taken place in the character of the world trading system since the nineteenth century, when most of the Western economies "took off." It would have been, on both political and economic grounds, a suicidal policy if Soviet Russia had expected to obtain through imports from the capitalist West the expanding capital requirements of her industrialization. Many underdeveloped countries today, faced with stagnant world demand for their primary exports and with tariff barriers for their light manufactures, seem to be finding the Soviet pattern of industrial development an increasingly attractive one to emulate.

Even if the view that international trade cannot be relied on to provide for the capital goods requirements of developing countries is accepted, it does not necessarily follow that these countries should expand current domestic production of capital goods to the fullest extent possible in the interest of growth. One reason for this is the fact that plant and equipment, once installed, became largely specific to the uses to which they have been committed. Thus if the objective of a long-term plan is to maximize consumer goods output at the terminal date, it is possible that the capital stock available for consumer goods production at that date would be smaller than it might have been—as a result of excessive investment in the capital goods industries in the earlier years of the plan—so that too much of the capital stock becomes specific to that sector.

It has, however, been shown by Mahalanobis (1953) and Domar (1957)—whose work is based on that of the Soviet economist Feldman in the 1920s—that the further the terminal date set for maximization of consumer goods output the greater should be the proportion of current investment allocated to the capital goods sector, in spite of the complete specificity of the capital stock once it is installed in either sector.

The Feldman-Domar-Mahalanobis model assumes that labor is not a scarce factor in the industrial sector. The justification for this assumption can no doubt be sought in the existence of "disguised unemployment" in the agricultural or, more generally, the "traditional" sector of the economy. This assumption alone, however, would not be sufficient. It has to be supplemented with the further assumptions that the state both wishes and is able, by force if necessary, to transfer any required amount of labor from the traditional sector, together with the means of subsistence that this labor would normally be consuming.

If either of these further assumptions is not satisfied, as for the most part they are not outside of the communist bloc of countries, labor could not be regarded as having zero real cost in the industrial sector in spite of "disguised unemployment" in agriculture. The level of industrial employment would depend on the quantity of manufactured consumer goods sold to the peasants in exchange for food, which is a crucial determinant of the "marketable surplus" in agriculture. The relationship between the accumulation of capital and the expansion of employment in the industrial sector therefore involves an essential "tradeoff," since more consumer goods to increase employment will divert resources from the capital goods branch of the industrial sector. This conflict over the allocation of investment between the two branches of the industrial sector is absent in the Feldman-Domar-Mahalanobis model and consequently requires further analysis.

One way of characterizing the Feldman-Domar-Mahalanobis model is to say that it is an "open" model in the sense that consumer goods only enter the model as "final demand." In a "closed" model, on the other hand, consumer goods are fed back into the productive process as inputs in the form of wage goods, the supply of which determines the size of the labor force that can be maintained. This aspect of "productive consumption" is of course familiar from Physiocratic, Ricardian, and Marxian economics and more recently in the closed version of the input-output model and the von Neumann (1945) general equilibrium growth model.

The Lewis (1954) model of economic development with unlimited supplies of labor is another instance of a closed model. As was mentioned in chapter 1 there is some ambiguity about the formal interpretation of the Lewis model, since he does not make explicit the exact structure of production assumed within the "modern" sector. One possible interpretation is that the output of this sector is a homogeneous manufactured consumer good, which can be exchanged for labor and food from the "traditional" sector at exogenously fixed rates. In this interpretation the reinvestment of profits takes the following form: the surplus in the consumer goods department becomes the wage bill or working capital for the labor that is employed in making capital goods for use in the consumer goods department. This implies that capital goods themselves are made by labor alone, since otherwise there would be the further problem of how investment and labor are to be allocated between machines to make consumer goods and "machines to make machines." Exactly the same model is used in two other well-known works, by Dobb (1960) and Sen (1960). This similarity has not been generally noticed, perhaps because Lewis uses marginal curves, Dobb average curves, and Sen total curves to exhibit the relationship between profit maximization and output maximization in the industrial sector.

We therefore have two opposite extremes in the nature of the assumptions about the production of capital goods: that labor can be ignored in the Feldman-Domar-Mahalanobis model and that capital can be ignored in the Lewis-Dobb-Sen model. Neither extreme is satisfactory. Our next objective, therefore, will be to construct models of development in a closed dual economy in which constraints on both labor and capital are operating on the "modern" or industrial sector and in which the tradeoff involved between relaxing one or the other is explicitly analyzed.

Here we shall assume that those in control of the industrial sector have the Stalinist objective of maximizing the output of capital goods, while considering consumer goods only to further promote the expansion of the capital goods sector. Some such conception must have been at the basis of the so-called Soviet "law of the superiority of heavy to light industry" and in view of the historical importance and continued relevance of this notion as a paradigm to the contemporary Third World, it would seem to be worth some analytical attention within the framework outlined above. Ultimately, of course, the intention would be to increase consumption, but the phase of building up a capital goods industry could conceivably last long enough for the means to become an end in itself.

II

The economic system to be considered is the industrial sector of an underdeveloped economy without foreign-trade relations, which draws its labor force and food supplies from an agricultural sector in which there is "disguised unemployment." We shall assume that there is a perfectly elastic supply of labor to the industrial sector at a fixed real wage in terms of food. The food to meet the wage bill of the industrial sector is obtained by selling manufactured consumer goods to the agricultural sector at fixed rates of exchange. Assuming that the propensity to save out of wages is zero and out of profits is unity, we have a condition in which the size of the labor force in the industrial sector is equal to the level of output of manufactured consumer goods divided by the real wage in terms of these goods. Since both the real wage in terms of food and the rate of exchange between food and manufactured consumables is fixed, the size of the industrial labor force is proportional to the level of output of the latter commodity.

Production of consumables in the industrial sector is by means of labor and capital goods which are produced in another department of the industrial sector by means of labor and capital goods. It is assumed that labor and the services of the capital goods can be substituted for each other in the production of each type of output. We assume no difference in the nature of those capital goods which are used to produce consumable goods and those which are used to produce more capital goods. As in the Feldman-Domar-Mahalanobis model, we assume that newly produced capital goods can be allocated to either sector, but that once installed they cannot be transferred. For simplicity we shall also assume that the capital goods do not depreciate.

In the initial period the stock of capital goods in each sector will be fixed, so that the output levels will depend only on the labor input. Since the capital goods sector depends upon the consumer goods sector for its labor force, the key variable in the short run is the level of production of consumer goods. At low levels of employment the marginal productivity of labor in this sector will exceed the fixed real wage, so that a surplus is earned. This surplus will go on increasing as employment in this sector is increased until the marginal productivity of labor is equal to the wage rate, at which point the surplus will be maximized, since further additions of labor will produce net losses. Thus, each worker in the consumer goods sector can be envisioned as feeding himself as well as providing a surplus with which to feed workers in the capital goods sector, assuming that the surplus is used exclusively for this purpose. Since in the short run the level of capital goods output depends only on the labor input, and this in turn on the surplus in the consumer goods sector, the relationship between the outputs of the two sectors will be as depicted by the *AA* curve in Fig. 2.1, where the point *X* corresponds to the surplus-maximizing level of consumer goods output. Points to the left of *X* should never be chosen, since the output of both sectors can be expanded. To the right of *X* the relative desirability of the two types of output have to be weighed against each other. If the objective is to maximize the output of capital goods the point X is the optimum. It should be noted that the level of the *AA* curve varies inversely with the real wage in terms of food and the rate of exchange between food and manufactured consumables.

For the determination of output levels in the next period the problem of allocating the capital goods produced between the two sectors in the initial period must be solved. If they are all installed in the consumer goods sector a given output of consumables will require less labor to produce it, so that the surplus available for feeding workers in the capital goods sector would be increased. With a given capital stock and more labor a larger output of capital goods could be produced for any given level of consumer goods output in the next period. In other words, the *AA* curve for the next period would lie above that of the initial period.

The upward shift of this curve, however, could be brought about in an entirely different way, by putting all the new capital goods into the capital goods sector itself. Then the surplus corresponding to a given output of consumables will be the same as in the initial period, since the capital stock in that sector remains unchanged; but the same amount of labor in the capital goods sector can now produce more output, since the capital stock in this sector is expanded. Which policy produces the greater upward shift of the *AA* curve cannot be determined *a priori*.

We have, however, considered only the two extreme cases. Corresponding to any division of the new capital goods between the two sectors, there will be one curve in the next period like the AA curve for the initial period. There will therefore be an infinity of such curves. Let A'A' in Fig. 2.1 be the envelope of all these curves and X' the point on the envelope at which the output of capital goods is at a maximum. Then the optimal investment allocation between the two sectors will be the one that generates the curve on which point X' lies. What are the conditions that determine point X' as the optimum? For the answer to this question we shall need a little mathematical analysis, which will be explained in common-sense terms afterwards.

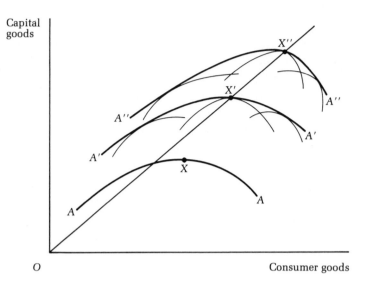

Figure 2.1

III

We shall use the following notation:

K	=	output of capital goods;
C	=	output of consumer goods;
L_k, L_c	=	labor employed in the production of capital goods and consumer goods respectively;
I_k, I_c	=	investment (services of capital goods produced in the previous period) allocated to the capital goods and consumer goods sectors respectively;
I	=	total available services of capital goods produced in the previous period;
w	=	wage rate in terms of consumer goods.

We have the following equations:

$$K = K(L_k, I_k) \tag{2.1}$$

$$C = C(L_c, I_c) \tag{2.2}$$

$$w(L_k + L_c) = C \qquad (2.3)$$

$$I_k + I_c = I \qquad (2.4)$$

Equations (2.1) and (2.2) are the production functions for the outputs of the two sectors, which are assumed to be of the neoclassical variety, with labor and capital continuously substitutable for each other at the margin. We put investment only instead of the total stock of capital into each production function because the existing capital stock in each sector is a constant and untransferable. Equation (2.3) expresses the fact that the total wage bill is equal to the output of consumer goods in this model, while equation (2.4) states that the sum of investment in the two sectors must be equal to the amount made possible by the output of capital goods in the previous period.

Since it will not cause any difficulty at the present stage, we may as well, for the sake of greater generality, assume that the real wage is a function of the demand for labor instead of being simply a constant, so that we have

$$w = f(L_k + L_c) \qquad (2.5)$$

The problem is to maximize the output of capital goods subject to these five equations. To do this we set up the Lagrangean expression

$$K(L_k, I_k) - \alpha[w(L_k + L_c) - C(L_c, I_c)] - \beta[I_k + I_c - I]$$

where α, β are Lagrangean multipliers. The necessary conditions for maximization are obtained by setting the partial derivatives of the Lagrangean expression equal to zero. After a little manipulation these conditions can be expressed as

$$\frac{\partial K}{\partial L_k} = \alpha w(1 + 1/E) \qquad (2.6)$$

$$\frac{\partial K}{\partial I_k} = \beta \qquad (2.7)$$

$$\frac{\partial C}{\partial L_c} = w(1 + 1/E) \qquad (2.8)$$

$$\frac{\partial C}{\partial I_c} = \frac{\beta}{\alpha} \tag{2.9}$$

where

$$E = \frac{w}{(L_k + L_c)} \frac{\partial L_k}{\partial w} = \frac{w}{(L_k + L_c)} \frac{\partial L_c}{\partial w} =$$

elasticity of supply of labor to the industrial sector.

This gives us exactly nine equations to solve for the seven variables K, C, L_c, L_k, I_c, I_k, w, and the two Lagrangean multipliers α and β.

From (27) and (29) it follows that

$$\alpha = \frac{\partial K}{\partial I_k} \cdot \frac{\partial I_c}{\partial C}$$

This shows that α is the marginal rate of transformation between capital goods and consumer goods, or the shadow price ratio of the two types of goods. The meaning of equations (2.6) and (2.8) is now clear. They are simply the well-known conditions for the optimal level of employment under monopsony; that the marginal value productivity of labor must be equal to the wage rate times a factor vàrying inversely with the elasticity of the supply of labor.

Substituting for α from (2.6), the relationship between the marginal productivities of capital in the two sectors implied by (2.7) and (2.9) is

$$\frac{\partial K}{\partial I_k} = \frac{\partial C}{\partial I_c} \cdot \frac{1}{w(1 + 1/E)} \cdot \frac{\partial K}{\partial L_k}$$

This condition can be given a very simple interpretation. Newly produced capital goods can contribute to the current output of capital goods in two ways. If they are installed in the capital goods sector itself they can raise production in that sector directly. The measure of how effectively this direct contribution can be made is the marginal productivity of capital in the capital goods sector, which is on the left-hand side of the equation. They may also, however, be installed in the consumer goods sector to increase the output there, and this additional output of consumer goods can be used to hire labor for employment in the capital goods sector, which is an alternative way of raising the output of capital goods. The effectiveness of this alternative method will depend upon the marginal productivity of capital in the consumer goods sector, the cost in terms of consumer goods of additional labor, and the marginal productivity of labor in producing capital goods. The right-hand side of the equation gives us just these three factors. Hence, we may interpret it as saying that for the production of capital goods to be at a maximum the "direct" marginal productivity of capital in producing capital goods must be equal to its "indirect" marginal productivity in the same use, by making additional labor available instead. This is very reminiscent of the example in Wicksell's *Lectures* of the man with a stock of corn which can be consumed directly or made into whisky. In order to maximize his utility he has to make sure that the marginal utility of corn consumed directly is equal to the marginal productivity of corn in making whisky multiplied by the marginal utility of whisky.

This condition clearly shows that it is possible for investment in the production of capital goods to the neglect of consumer goods to be self-defeating, because a diversion of investment to the consumer goods sector could yield not only more consumer goods but more capital goods as well, by making it possible to employ additional labor in that sector so as to more than compensate for the reduction in investment. This possibility does not arise in the Feldman-Domar-Mahalanobis model because of its assumption that labor is not a scarce factor. The assumption on which the present analysis is based is, of course, that capital and labor can be substituted for each other in the production of both types of goods, at least over a certain range.

An alternative way of writing the condition above is

$$\frac{\partial L_k}{\partial K} \cdot \frac{\partial K}{\partial I_k} = \frac{\partial C}{\partial I_c} \cdot \frac{1}{w(1 + 1/E)}$$

The left-hand side is the marginal rate of substitution between labor and capital in producing capital goods. If we assume that there is a perfectly elastic supply of labor at a fixed real wage, the elasticity factor will disappear from the equation so that the right-hand side will be equal to the marginal productivity of capital in the consumer goods sector divided by the real wage. If constant returns to scale in both sectors are assumed the real wage and the marginal productivity of capital in the consumer goods sector will vary inversely, so that the marginal rate of substitution between labor and capital in the capital goods sector will also vary inversely with the real wage. Therefore, the more capital-intensive techniques are chosen in the capital goods sector, the higher is the real wage rate.

IV

The institutional pattern of the economic system has not so far been specified. The analysis can readily be seen to be consistent, however, with either socialist planning or competitive capitalism, if the real wage is taken as fixed. This is because maximizing profit and maximizing the output of capital goods amount to the same thing if all wages are consumed and all profits are invested, which is what is implied by equation (2.3). The optimization conditions of equations (2.6) through (2.9), when E is infinite, are simply the familiar conditions of profit maximization under perfect competition: that the marginal value productivity of a factor be equal to its price. The Lagrangean multiplier β is the rental of new capital goods, in terms of capital goods, and the other one α was earlier seen to be the marginal rate of transformation between the two types of outputs.

The Lagrangeans would thus be market prices if competitive capitalism prevailed, accounting prices if Lange-Lerner decentralized socialism prevailed, or electronically computed shadow prices if central planning in the manner of Kantorovich prevailed. Their values are determined purely by the objective and the technology and are quite independent of the form of the economic regime. "Accumulate! Accumulate!" can be Moses and the prophets to planners just as much as to capitalists.

V

If one supposes that the output of capital goods is maximized in each period according to the optimal principles laid down above, the characteristics of the time path, or "trajectory," along which the system evolves over successive periods will be very difficult to determine if the problem is tackled in full generality. We shall therefore assume that the real wage rate is fixed and that there are constant returns to scale in both sectors.

Since capital is being accumulated, the curves showing the relationships between the output levels of the two sectors, as in Fig. 2.1, will lie successively one above the other as time goes on. The diagram for the evolution of the system can be obtained by joining the peaks of each of these successive curves, since these peaks correspond to the maximum output of capital goods in each period.

We shall first prove that each of these peaks will lie to the right of the preceding one, meaning that consumer goods output also grows over time as a consequence of maximizing the output of capital goods. To see this consider the point on the tth period's curve that lies directly above the peak of the curve for period $t-1$. So long as there is any investment at all in the consumer goods sector the capital stock will be larger in the later period and, since the output of consumer goods is the same, the marginal productivity of labor must be higher. The real wage rate is, however, the same by hypothesis, so that the peak of the later period's curve must lie not only above but also to the right of the peak for the earlier period. This is because equation (2.8) requires the marginal productivity of labor in the consumer goods sector to be equal to the real wage rate if E is infinite, as is now assumed.

Since the real wage rate is fixed and there are constant returns to scale in both sectors, the choice of techniques or input coefficients will remain unchanged from period to period in spite of there always being the technical possibility of capital-labor substitution. This is because equation (2.8) always requires the marginal productivity of labor in the consumer goods sector to be equal to the fixed real wage rate and, with constant returns to scale, this

requires the capital-labor ratio in the consumer goods sector always to remain unchanged. Equations (2.6) through (2.9) can also
be seen to imply that the ratios of the marginal productivities of
capital and labor in the two sectors must be equal, and this, if
there are constant returns to scale in the capital goods sector, can
be the case only if the capital-labor ratio in that sector also
remains fixed.

With input coefficients fixed, output and the wage bill in the
consumer goods sector, and therefore the surplus as well, will all
expand at the same rate. Since the labor force in the capital goods
sector is proportional to the surplus in the consumer goods sector,
this will also expand at the same rate; and since the input coefficients in the capital goods sector also remain unchanged, this
means that the outputs of the two sectors grow at the same rate. It
thus follows that adherence to the optimization rules in successive periods generates a balanced growth path for the system. In
terms of Fig. 2.1 this is shown by the fact that the points X', and X''
lie on the same line through the origin. The point X is not placed
on this line, since the historically given proportion between the
capital stocks of the two sectors will not generally be the optimum
one.

The balanced growth relation can be written as

$$\frac{\Delta K}{K} = \frac{\Delta C}{C}$$

from which it follows simply that

$$\frac{\Delta K}{\Delta C} = \frac{K}{C}$$

which shows that the increments to production in each sector
must be in a fixed ratio to each other. With input coefficients fixed
for the reasons explained above we can write:

$$\frac{\Delta K}{\Delta C} = \frac{x_1 I_k}{x_2 I_c}$$

where x_1, x_2 indicate the constant incremental output-capital
ratios in the two sectors. From this it follows that the ratio of in-

vestment in the two sectors to each other must also remain fixed. Let y_1 denote the fixed proportion of total investment directed to the capital goods sector. Then, since the total investment in the tth period is equal to the output of capital goods in the $(t-1)$ period, we can write

$$K_{t+1} - K_t = x_1 y_1 K_t$$

$$K_t - K_{t-1} = x_1 y_1 K_{t-1}$$

From which it follows that

$$\frac{K_{t+1} - K_t}{K_t} = \frac{K_t - K_{t-1}}{K_{t-1}} = x_1 y_1$$

This shows that the balanced growth takes place at a constant rate equal to the product of the incremental output–capital ratio and the share of total investment of the capital goods sector. This expression for the growth rate is similar to that of the Feldman-Domar-Mahalanobis model, with the difference that x_1 is taken as given in their model, whereas its optimal value is chosen in ours.

VI

We have shown that if the production of capital goods is maximized in each period the time path that results for the system as a whole is balanced growth at a steady rate along the line $OX'X''$ in Fig. 2.1. We shall now show that this balanced-growth path followed by the system is the *maximal* balanced growth path; i.e., the rate of steady growth along this path is greater than for any other balanced-growth path.

In order to demonstrate this result, let us assume that the desideratum is maximization of the rate of growth of capital goods output rather than of its level in each period, and that the technological and behavioral constraints remain the same. In this case the maximization problem can be written as

Maximize $$\frac{K_t}{K_{t-1}}$$

Subject to

$$K_t = K(L_{Kt}, I_{Kt}); \quad K_{t-1} = K(L_{Kt-1}, I_{Kt-1})$$

$$Ct = C(L_{ct}, I_{ct}); \quad C_{t-1} = C(L_{ct-1}, I_{ct-1})$$

$$w(L_{ct} + L_{Kt}) = C_t; \quad w(L_{ct-1} + L_{Kt-1}) = C_{t-1}$$

$$I_{Kt} + I_{ct} \pm K_{t-1}; \quad I_{Kt-1} + I_{ct-1} = I$$

The Lagrangean expression is

$$\frac{K_t}{K_{t-1}} - \alpha[w(L_{ct-1} + L_{kt-1}) - C_{t-1}] - \beta[w(L_{ct} + L_{kt}) - C_t]$$

$$-\phi[I_{kt} + I_{ct} - K_{t-1}] - \lambda[I_{Kt-1} + I_{ct-1} - I]$$

where α, β, ϕ and λ are Lagrangean multipliers. Setting the partial derivatives of this expression equal to zero to obtain the necessary conditions for maximization, we have

$$\frac{1}{K_{t-1}} \frac{\partial K_t}{\partial L_{Kt}} - \beta w = 0 \qquad (2.10)$$

$$\frac{1}{K_{t-1}} \frac{\partial K_t}{\partial I_{Kt}} - \phi = 0 \qquad (2.11)$$

$$-\frac{K_t}{K^2_{t-1}} \frac{\partial K_{t-1}}{\partial L_{Kt-1}} - \alpha w + \phi \frac{\partial K_{t-1}}{\partial L_{Kt-1}} = 0 \qquad (2.12)$$

$$-\frac{K_t}{K^2_{t-1}} \frac{\partial K_{t-1}}{\partial I_{Kt-1}} + \phi \frac{\partial K_{t-1}}{\partial I_{Kt-1}} - \lambda = 0 \qquad (2.13)$$

$$-\alpha w + \alpha \frac{\partial C_{t-1}}{\partial L_{ct-1}} = 0 \qquad (2.14)$$

$$-\beta w + \beta \frac{\partial C_t}{\partial L_{ct}} = 0 \qquad (2.15)$$

$$\frac{\alpha \, \partial C_{t-1}}{\partial I_{ct-1}} - \lambda = 0 \qquad (2.16)$$

$$\beta \frac{\partial C_t}{\partial I_{ct}} - \phi = 0 \qquad (2.17)$$

Together with the eight constraint equations, we have exactly enough equations to determine the unknowns. After elimination of the Lagrangean multipliers equations (2.10) through (2.17) can be written as

$$\frac{\partial C_t}{\partial L_{ct}} = w$$

$$\frac{\partial C_{t-1}}{\partial L_{ct-1}} = w$$

$$\frac{\partial K_t}{\partial I_{Kt}} = \frac{\partial C_t}{\partial I_{ct}} \cdot \frac{1}{w} \cdot \frac{\partial K_t}{\partial L_{Kt}}$$

$$\frac{\partial K_{t-1}}{\partial I_{Kt-1}} = \frac{\partial C_{t-1}}{\partial I_{ct-1}} \cdot \frac{1}{w} \cdot \frac{\partial K_{t-1}}{\partial L_{Kt-1}}$$

It can be seen that these conditions are identical with the ones obtained earlier for the maximization of the level of capital goods output in each period. Hence, in the present model maximizing the rate of growth of capital goods output and maximizing the level in each period amount to the same thing. Since we have already seen that the latter objective generates a balanced growth path, it now follows that this balanced-growth path is the one with the maximum rate of steady growth—or the von Neumann path, as it is customary to call it.

Observing that

$$\frac{K_t}{K_{t-1}} = (1 + g)$$

where g is the rate of growth of capital-goods output, it follows from the condition that all profits are invested and all wages are consumed that

$$g = \frac{\partial K_t}{\partial I_{Kt}}$$

The maximal rate of balanced growth is therefore equal to the marginal productivity of captial in the capital goods sector. We may also interpret the right-hand side as the rate of interest, so that we have the well-known proposition that the rate of growth will be equal to the rate of interest in a "closed" model where all consumer goods output is input for producing labor.

The result can be given an intuitive explanation by means of the familiar elementary proposition that average product must equal marginal product when the former is at a maximum. K_t/K_{t-1} can be looked upon as the average product of capital goods in producing new capital goods, and so it follows that for this to be maximized it must be equal to the marginal product of capital in making new capital goods plus unity, or the gross marginal product of capital.

The effect of a rise in the real wage rate on the rate of growth can now be ascertained. From the optimization conditions it follows that the marginal productivity of labor in the consumer goods sector will rise if the real wage rate rises and, because of constant returns to scale, this means that the marginal productivity of capital in the consumer goods sector will fall. The optimization conditions imply that the ratios of the marginal productivities of labor and capital in the two sectors are equal. Hence, if the ratio rises in the consumer goods sector it must also rise in the capital-goods sector, and because of constant returns to scale this can happen only if the marginal productivity of capital in the capital goods sector falls. Since we have seen that the rate of growth of the system is equal to this marginal productivity it follows that the rate of growth varies inversely with the real wage rate.

VII

The main result of our analysis has been to show that even if the objective of planning is to maximize the level or rate of growth of capital goods output the optimal allocation of investment requires the output of consumer goods to expand at the same rate as capital goods output, as a result of the role of "productive consumption" in the model. It would therefore seem that there would be little justification for any "law of superiority of heavy industry to light industry."

It is, however, possible that all the investment has to be put into the capital goods sector. This would be the case where even after all the investment has been put into the capital goods sector the "direct" marginal productivity of capital in producing capital goods is greater than the "indirect" marginal productivity. In this case the peaks of the successive curves in Figure 2.1 will be vertically above each other, indicating a growth path in which the output of capital goods only is expanding, while that of consumer goods is stationary. This growth path cannot continue indefinitely, however, since with a constant labor force and an expanding capital stock in the capital goods sector the "direct" marginal productivity of capital will be falling over time, and as more and more new capital goods become available for investment in successive periods there must come a time when it pays to put some investment into the consumer goods sector to get more labor for the capital goods sector. Once this happens, the growth path will no longer be vertical, but will be along a ray through the origin—i.e. there is balanced growth. As was proved earlier, this balanced growth path will be maximal.

Given the technology and initial capital stocks the likelihood of an initial unbalanced phase in the growth process is greater the higher is the real wage rate, since this makes for a lower indirect marginal productivity of capital in producing capital goods. Alternatively, given the wage rate the relative magnitude of the direct and indirect marginal productivities will depend on the proportion of the initial capital stocks in the two sectors. If the capital stock in the capital goods sector is relatively low, the direct marginal productivity of capital will be high there, which makes it more likely that it can absorb all the investment initially until the optimal proportion is reached, after which balanced growth takes place. This situation may apply in underdeveloped economies, offsetting the influence of a low wage rate in the opposite direction, and thus justifying the "law of superiority of heavy industry to light industry."

We may note that since the objective of maximizing capital goods in each period puts the economy either immediately or eventually on to the von Neumann path, this means that in the long run there will be not only greater capital goods production but also greater consumer goods production, and hence employment as well, than if a path immediately more favorable to consumption and employment were chosen. For example, if it were desired to draw off the "disguised unemployment" from the agricultural sector in the shortest possible time, the best way of doing it might be to follow the von Neumann path instead of another that gave more employment at the beginning. Stoleru (1965) gives a rigorous analysis of such a problem in terms of the Feldman-Domar-Mahalanobis model, which is to say that labor is not a scarce factor and there is no "productive consumption," which is the essential feature of the model given here.

The celebrated "turnpike theorem" of Dorfman, Samuelson, and Solow (1958) demonstrated that, under certain conditions, the best way to reach *any* sufficiently long-run objective on terminal capital stocks or output levels was to follow the von Neumann path for most of the way. The crude Stalinist planner who blindly maximizes capital goods output in each period on the basis of a dogmatic "law of superiority of heavy industry to light industry" might therefore be led after all by an "invisible hand" to promote an end that was no part of his intention.

An examination of development planning in a closed dual economy in terms of the "turnpike" approach is attempted in the next chapter, which will also relax the assumptions of an exogenously fixed wage rate and terms of trade that have been made here.

CHAPTER 3

Intertemporal Efficiency and Developmental Planning

THE DISCUSSION of the relationship between capital accumulation and "productive consumption" is continued in this chapter, with modifications of some of the structural assumptions, by means of an adapted geometric version of the Dorfman-Samuelson-Solow "turnpike" model.

I

We shall continue to consider the modern sector to be divided into two branches, which produce manufactured consumer goods and capital goods respectively. The former will be called "textiles" and the latter "machines." Each of these outputs is assumed to be produced under conditions represented by constant-returns-to-scale, neoclassical production functions, with labor and capital (services from machines) as the inputs. Foreign trade continues to be excluded. The main difference from the model of chapter 2 is in the specification of the traditional sector. With a fixed wage in terms of food and also a fixed relative price of food to manufactured consumer goods the real wage in terms of the latter is a constant, which of course greatly simplifies the analysis but at the cost of neglecting some important aspects of the relations between the two sectors in the process of development.

Just as the modern sector in the specification adopted can be identified as "industry" the traditional sector in the present chapter will be considered as "agriculture," which produces a single homogeneous output to be called "corn." The labor force of peasants in agriculture is assumed to be so large in relation to the available land and equipment that there would be zero marginal productivity of labor if each peasant family worked the full number of hours it is willing to. The implication of this is that if some members find jobs in industry the remaining people would work harder and keep total output of corn at the same level. Remuneration to individual members of the homogeneous peasant families in agriculture is assumed to be equal to the average product of labor in producing corn.

Time will be divided into discrete "periods." The form of the supply function for labor to industry is taken as perfectly elastic at a level equal to the average productivity of labor in agriculture in the preceding period. Thus, although always perfectly elastic, the level of the supply curve of labor to industry can shift from period to period depending on what happens to total corn output and the labor force in agriculture. Total corn output, by the "disguised unemployment" assumption, is exogenously determined in the model. It can be made to increase over time as a result of increases in the supply of land or improvements in technology so long as the marginal product of labor continues to be zero. Population growth will tend to make this situation persist.

Wages are paid to labor in terms of corn at the start of each period. With an initial stock of machines and corn, which can be exchanged for labor at an initially fixed corn wage, the endowments of capital and labor for industry are determined. Together with the technology this specifies the alternative combinations of textiles and new machines that can be produced. The latter are not available for addition to the effective capital stock until the beginning of the next period. Both new and previously installed machines will be assumed to be freely shiftable from machines to textiles in contrast to the more realistic assumption of limited flexibility made in chapter 2. The only use that industry has for textiles is to exchange it with agriculture for corn with which to hire labor. In this way industry is a closed system in which an ini-

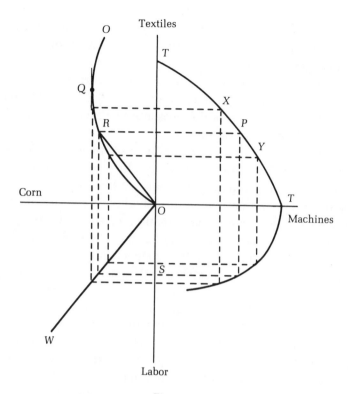

Figure 3.1

tial combination of capital and labor can be made to accumulate over time in various alternative proportions. Industry is regarded as being controlled by a single centralized planning authority, although it is possible that there is decentralized management and allocation in the Lange-Lerner fashion.

Industry's demand for labor has now to be introduced. This is best done with reference to Figure 3.1. *TT* represents the transformation curve in industry between the production of machines and textiles. Production takes place with a given initial stock of machines and an initial level of employment of labor, wages having been paid out of an initial fund of corn.

OO is the offer curve for textiles in exchange for corn. It is identical with the Marshallian offer curve, a familiar tool in the theory of international trade. The slope of a vector from the origin to *OO* represents a price ratio and the coordinates of the point at which it intersects OO indicate the quantities of corn and textiles that will be exchanged at that price ratio. Since it is assumed that the wage bill in terms of corn is paid at the start of the current period, as in the "advances to labor" of the Physiocrats and Ricardo, OO represents the offer not only of the peasants in agriculture but of the workers in industry as well.

The planning authority, being in the position of a pure monopolist, can select the point on OO that is to its greatest advantage. The authority, in making its decision, will refer to some conjectured offer curve rather than to the actual one, OO. Discrepancies will arise due to errors in anticipating exactly what the actual offer curve is. In practice this would be a very important problem, but since it is only the logic of the process that is the concern here, it is assumed that the conjectured and actual offer curves always coincide.

Any decision as to the quantity of textiles produced—i.e., the choice of a point on OO—at the same time determines a point on TT and hence the output of new machines. As the output of textiles rises from zero, the corn proceeds from their exchange increase also, but the output of new machines declines. At the point Q on OO the corn proceeds reach a maximum. It follows that textile outputs above those corresponding to Q on OO will never be chosen since they imply both less corn and fewer new machines. Up to the point Q, however, a choice has to be made between the relative desirability of corn and machines, since more of one can only be obtained at the expense of less of the other.

Machines are desired solely for their use in production. Corn could be desired for consumption by the state authorities but, since this use is not likely to be an important one, it is simplest to ignore it altogether. Therefore the sole reason the state has for acquiring corn is to meet the wage bill for the subsequent period.[1]

---

[1]The simplifying assumption that all stocks of corn held by industry at the start of a period are expended on labor in that period itself is made in order to keep the problem manageable. It is also assumed that textiles are not hoarded from one period to another but are exchanged for corn in the same period as they are produced.

Corn is thus a factor of production at one remove. This is displayed in the southwest quadrant of Figure 3.1. OW represents the wage rate for the current period determined by labor's average productivity in agriculture in the previous period. Obviously, the more corn the state can acquire, the greater the number of workers it can employ in the next period. The maximum employment possible in industry is determined by the point Q on OO. The curve in the southeast quadrant shows the possible combinations of labor and new machines that can be chosen for the next period.[2]

It now becomes perfectly obvious that nothing can be decided concerning the current allocation of resources between textiles and machines until some criterion is introduced that will take account of the future, since alternative choices of the current machine-textiles mix will give alternative factor endowment patterns to subsequent periods.

This criterion is assumed to be provided in the form of a function showing combinations of machines and textiles output between which the state is indifferent, and the decision rule is taken to be the maximization of this function over some specified time-horizon.[3] Thus a set of curves could be drawn in machines-textiles space and the problem of industry conceived as pushing the transformation curve out as far as possible so as to be tangential to the highest "social indifference curve." For simplicity these curves are assumed to be either convex or straight lines. The latter case would correspond to maximizing national income in industry at some socially determined fixed price ratio between machines and textiles.

The locus of possible factor endowments for the next period is readily derived from the curve in the southeast quadrant of Figure 3.1. The existing stock of machines can be added to the new

[2]The convexity of this curve follows from that of the transformation and offer curves.

[3]This procedure is of course highly arbitrary, since the valuations of the two goods in the terminal period will depend on their uses in further time periods. This is perhaps the most fundamental problem confronting the theory of capital, with the exception of considerations relating to uncertainty. Frank Ramsey's well-known solution to the problem was to take the terminal point as determined either by utility satiation or technical saturation.

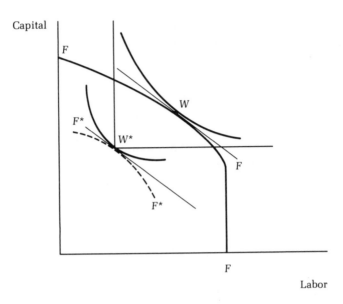

Figure 3.2

machines produced and the total amount of capital thereby obtained. The FF curve in Figure 3.2 indicates the pattern of factor
endowments possible for the next period.

From the FF curve it is possible to derive the production possibilities or transformation curve between machines and textiles for
the next period. This curve would differ from the one most familiar to economists since factor endowments are variable instead of
being fixed as in the usual derivation from the Edgeworth-Bowley
box diagram. The method of construction in the present case, as
depicted in Figure 3.2, is as follows. Take the isoquant for any
specified level of the output of one commodity. Slide this
isoquant along the FF curve in such a way that it is always tangential to it. The point of origin of the isoquant diagram will then
trace out a locus within the FF curve that is labelled F^*F^*. This
locus shows the quantity of each factor available after various possible factor combinations to produce the specified output have
been subtracted from the total factor availabilities. The isoquant
map for the other commodity can then be superimposed on Figure

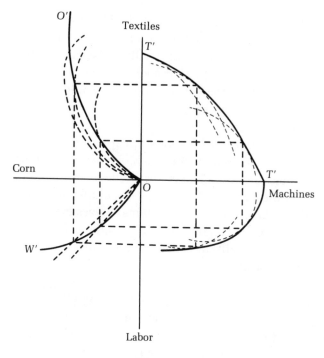

Figure 3.3

3.2 and the point on F^*F^* that is tangential to the highest isoquant determines the factor endowment that maximizes the output of one commodity given the output of the other. Once the point on F^*F^* is obtained, the origin of the isoquant diagram for the commodity the output of which is specified can be set so as to coincide with it, and the point of tangency between the isoquant for the specified output and FF gives the optimal total factor endowment.

An Edgeworth-Bowley box with the dimensions selected in this fashion can then be set up and a production-possibilities curve derived from it. Thus for each specified level of one output there will be a unique production-possibilites curve, and the envelope of all these curves constitutes the production frontier for society in the next period, as indicated by $T'T'$ in Figure 3.3.

Every point on $T'T'$ corresponds to a point on TT that generates the factor endowments that make it attainable. Every point on TT, however, does not correspond to a point on T'T'. This is shown by the following argument. Consider the FF curve in Figure 3.2. Suppose that the output of either good was set at zero. Then the maximum amount of the other good that could be produced would be determined by the tangency of FF with an isoquant for that commodity. In this case FF and F*F* coincide. Let us suppose further that one of the goods is capital-intensive and the other labor-intensive (which one is which does not matter) in the Lerner-Samuelson sense.[4] The factor endowment that maximizes the output of the capital-intensive good will therefore have more capital and less labor than that which maximizes the output of the labor-intensive good. The optimal factor endowment for any mix of both the goods will thus lie between these limits. Corresponding to these two limiting points on FF there will be two points on TT indicated by X and Y. It is therefore only the points on TT lying on the XY segment that generate all the points on T'T'. Points to the left of X and to the right of Y will never be chosen, since the factor endowments that they determine for the next period will be suboptimal for any output mix in that period.

II

It has thus been shown that, given the initial endowments of labor and capital in industry, the offer curve of workers and peasants, and the supply curve of labor, it is possible to describe the production frontier for industry in the next period, assuming no change in technology. If any point on T'T' is specified as a target for industry, a point on TT can be found that will provide just enough of both factors to make the target point attainable.

Suppose, however, that a target were set for industry not in terms of the next period's output mix but of any finite number of periods away. Will it then still be possible to determine a point on TT such that the target is attained? At the outset, there does not seem to be any difficulty in doing this. It has already been shown

[4]See Lerner (1952) and Samuelson (1949).

that given *TT, OO,* and *OW* it is possible to obtain *T'T'*, the production frontier for the next period. Given corresponding offer curves and supply curves, the production possibilities curves of the additional periods could be derived in the same way that *T'T'* was. If the objective is maximization of the given preference function over the specified number of periods, the point of tangency between the production-possibilities curve for the last period and the highest attainable social indifference curve would determine the outputs of the target period and its optimal factor endowment. In order to make the target point attainable, a unique point on the production-possibilities curve of the preceding period will have to be chosen, and this in turn will involve a unique point on all previous curves until the optimal point on *TT* is reached.

The process of generating successive production-possibilities curves, however, encounters what appears to be a serious obstacle as soon as one attempts to proceed from *T'T'* to the curves for later periods. This is because the offer curve and labor supply curve, which together with *T'T'* determine the locus of possible factor endowments for the next period, cannot be given independently of the choice of outputs for the initial period.

In Figure 3.1, as the output of textiles is substituted for that of machines, the corn proceeds increase up to the level of textiles output corresponding to the point *Q* on *OO*. This means that employment in industry in the next period will rise as we proceed along *TT* in the direction of greater textiles output. The more people there are in industry, the less there will be in agriculture. On the one hand this makes for increasing per capita real income in agriculture, since there are fewer individuals among whom any given output is to be shared. On the other hand, total output might fall. It shall be assumed, however, that the "disguised unemployment" and the increase in population is so large that the maximal withdrawal of labor into industry still leaves the marginal productivity of labor zero in agriculture.

Thus the average corn productivity of labor in the initial period, and hence the real wage to industry in the next period, increases as textiles are substituted for machines along the "efficient" *XY* segment of *TT*. Since each point on *T'T'* corresponds to a unique point on this segment, the real wage in the next period will be different for each point on $T'T'$. Whether it rises or falls as textiles are substituted for machines along $T'T'$ depends upon the assumptions regarding the relative factor intensities of the two goods. If textiles were the labor-intensive commodity, the real wage would rise as textiles were substituted for machines along $T'T'$. If the factor intensities were reversed, the opposite would happen. In either case there would be a family of straight wage-rate lines in the southwest quadrant of Figure 3.3 instead of the single line in Figure 3.1. Each one of these lines would correspond to one of the transformation curves enveloped by $T'T'$.

The position and shape of the next period's offer curve is also dependent on the decision for the current period. The more the current output-mix favors textiles, the greater will be the quantity of corn in the hands of peasants and workers in the next period. This is because the quantity of corn that is in their hands is equal to the next period's harvest, which, because of the "disguised unemployment" assumption, is independent of decisions in industry, and the industrial wage bill for the next period, which is an inventory carryover from the current period that increases as textiles are substituted for machines in the current output mix of industry.

Therefore, corresponding to each point on $T'T'$ there will be an entire offer curve which shows the reciprocal supply and demand at various alternative price ratios for a given real income of workers and peasants in terms of corn. As textiles are substituted for Machines along $T'T'$ this real income either increases or decreases continually, depending upon the relative factor intensities of the two goods. On the assumption that textiles are not inferior goods, the offer curves will either lie increasingly farther out or farther in as textiles are substituted for machines, depending upon whether real income is rising or falling during the process. The fact that the offer curve is shifting from point to point in this way seems to introduce an essential indeterminacy into the picture.

This, however, is by no means necessarily the case, as will be shown by the following argument. Suppose that the tastes of workers and peasants as a group could be adequately represented by a system of indifference curves that have the usual "well-behaved" properties, and that these tastes were known to the planning authority. Then, for any given real income in terms of corn an offer curve could be derived showing the reciprocal supply and demand at each price ratio. Since each level of textile output implies a certain level of real income in terms of corn, an offer curve could be drawn for each such level of textile output. Thus a family of offer curves is generated in the northwest quadrant of Figure 3.3 instead of a single curve as in Figure 3.1. For each transformation curve enveloped by $T'T'$ there is a corresponding unique offer curve and wage-rate line. For any level of textiles output the real income, and hence the offer curve, is known so that the price ratio that clears the market can be located on the offer curve. The locus of all such points for each level of textile output could be drawn to form a "composite" offer curve OO' along which not only the price-ratio but real income as well would vary. Similarly OW' is the "composite wage-rate line." Figure 3.3 is drawn on the assumption that textiles are the labor-intensive good.

Thus no indeterminacy exists. For each point on $T'T'$ the corn proceeds and the wage rate are known so that a curve showing the possible combinations of new machines and labor that could be used in the next period can be drawn in the southeast quadrant of Figure 3.3. This curve is the envelope of all the curves that could be drawn for each of the transformation curves enveloped by $T'T'$. Factor endowments, and hence production possibilities, for the next period, can now be derived. Passage to subsequent periods presents no additional problems, since the analysis for the second period would still apply without modification.

The problem of what the current allocation of resources between textiles and machines should be can now be solved, given the preference function which is to be maximized over any specified number of periods. This is because the terminal position of industry is arrived at by the tangency of the last period's transformation curve with the highest social indifference curve, and that implies a unique path to this position. The production point on the initial transformation curve thus determined generates a particular transformation curve for the next period, and, the production point on this and all subsequent curves being determined as well, the evolution to the optimal terminal position is completely described. In the process, the terms of trade between textiles and corn and the real wage of labor are determined for each period, together with the capital and labor in each sector of industry. The failure to be at the "correct" point on any of the intervening periods' transformation curves would make the optimal terminal position unattainable.

The problem that was posed has therefore been solved, not without paying the price of making certain strong restrictive assumptions. The major one is, of course, the fact that industry is assumed to be able to predict with perfect accuracy the tastes of workers and peasants, total output in agriculture, the total population, and the supply curve of labor.

It would be wrong to criticize the model as unrealistic if it were considered simply as the framework for economic planning, since, in some way or another, the authorities would have to estimate the necessary information about the behavior of the workers and peasants. Once the plans have been adopted and put into effect, however, errors in forecasting are bound to appear. How the system would respond to these errors is not investigated at all here. It therefore cannot serve as a "behavioral" model of a planned economy. Only if all forecasts turn out to be perfectly correct would it actually turn out to be a descriptive model. It is therefore not so much "unrealistic" as incomplete, in the sense that there are no prescribed reaction mechanisms for incorrect forecasting built into the system. This, in the present state of knowledge, seems to be true of all models that involve optimization over time.

A system of shadow prices, or "duals" in linear programming terminology, can now be derived. These could be used for the Lange-Lerner type decentralization of decisions involving the implementation of the optimal plan. As the reader familiar with modern economic theory knows, these shadow prices are essentially marginal rates of substitution of various kinds between inputs and outputs.

In Figure 3.1, suppose that the point P on TT is the one at which it is necessary to produce in order to realize the plan. The slope of TT at P, or the marginal rate of transformation at that point between textiles and machines, is the shadow price ratio of the two outputs for the first period. Since every point on TT corresponds to a point on the "efficiency locus" of the box diagram from which TT is derived, the shadow price ratio of labor and capital is determined as the common marginal rate of substitution between these factors in producing the two outputs. P also determines the terms of trade between corn and textiles measured in Figure 3.1 by the slope of OR. This would not be a shadow price ratio but an observable market price ratio. Employment for the next period is determined as OS, so that the factor endowment for the next period can be specifically located as a point, labelled W, on the curve FF in Figure 3.2. The slope of FF at W measures the marginal rate at which the capital and labor that the current period bequeaths to the next can be transformed into each other. All price ratios of the first period have therefore been determined.

Since the optimal point on $T'T'$ is also known, the process described for ascertaining the shadow price ratios in the first period could be repeated for the second and all subsequent periods. As one might well suspect, the shadow price ratios for the first and for all subsequent periods are inextricably linked: Since P is the optimal point on TT, W is the optimal point on FF, because it represents the optimal factor endowment for the optimal point on $T'T'$. Corresponding to W on FF will be the point W^* on F^*F^*, which determines the optimal amount of capital and labor to be used in producing the output, which is to be maximized subject to some specified level of the other output. It does not, of course, matter which good is held fixed and which is maximized. The slope of F^*F^* at W^*, which indicates the marginal rate of substitution between labor and capital in producing the good the output of which is to be maximized, must be equal to the slope of FF at W, which measures the rate at which labor is substituted for capital in producing the other good. But the slope of *FF* at *W* also measures the rate at which capital can be transformed into labor in the first period for use in the second. Thus the shadow factor-price ratio for the second period is connected with the corresponding ratio for the first period and hence with the shadow product-price ratio. The product-price ratio for the second period will be given by the one-to-one correspondence that exists between it and the factor-price ratio. In this way the whole system of shadow prices is linked over time. The crucial intertemporal efficiency condition that provides the link is the equality between the marginal rate of substitution between capital and labor in the *t*th period and the marginal rate of transformation between them in the $t - 1$ th period.

III

The analysis of the previous sections of the paper has determined (by an adaptation of the Dorfman-Samuelson-Solow turnpike model to fit the circumstances considered) a development path that reconciles, for any particular objective specified, the two conflicting requirements of industrialization in a backward economy: the expansion of capital goods production and the transfer of manpower from the agricultural sector. This development path generates for each period the optimal choices for the terms of trade with the agricultural sector and the techniques of production to be adopted in the capital and consumer goods departments of the industrial sector.

The problem of choice of technique has been extensively studied in the development literature, with the most comprehensive contributions being those of Maurice Dobb (1960) and A. K. Sen (1960). The advance made here over the work of these authors is to convert the industrial real wage and the terms of trade between agriculture and industry from parameters to variables determined simultaneously with the choice of both the pattern and techniques of production within a general equilibrium model. Choice of techniques is thus determined with reference to the entire process of planned development rather than analyzed in isolation as an aspect of that process. Another noteworthy difference from the work of Dobb and Sen is that techniques are not chosen once and for all over the entire horizon but are free to vary from period to period up to the horizon as efficiency dictates.

It is interesting to note that Arthur Lewis's (1955) recommendation that the terms of trade should be kept stable over time would lead to a deviation from the optimum path.[5] The view of the terms of trade emerging from the present model seems rather to be that of the Soviet economist Preobrazhensky who, in the 1920s, advocated setting the terms of trade with the rural sector so as to maximize "primitive socialist accumulation."[6]

The conflict between investment in the consumer goods sector and in the capital goods sector due to the specificity of the capital stock is resolved by the Feldman-Domar-Mahalanobis model—regardless of the desired composition of output at the horizon—increasingly in favor of the capital goods sector as the length of the horizon is extended. The present model has analyzed an entirely different ground of conflict, because of the necessity of consumer goods production to obtain labor, which is ignored by those authors. It would therefore be interesting and important to see whether a similar resolution can also be arrived at in the present case.

In deriving the transformation curve $T'T'$ from TT it was shown that all points on $T'T'$ were generated only from points on the XY segment of TT. The possibility can therefore arise, as it cannot in the Feldman-Domar-Mahalanobis model, that the production of machines will be excessive: less machines and more textiles in the current period could increase the output of both items in the next period. As the horizon is extended one period further into the future the segment of efficient points on TT would lie within XY itself, since the choice of points on $T'T'$ would now also be restricted to an intermediate segment, that necessary to generate $T''T''$. It can readily be seen that further extensions of the horizon would narrow the efficient segment on TT even more. Thus, as in

---

[5]See Lewis (1955) p. 276.
[6]See Erlich (1950) for a discussion.

the Feldman-Domar-Mahalanobis model, the longer the horizon the less acute becomes the conflict between consumer goods and capital goods production. Unlike that model, however, the conflict is not always resolved in favor of capital goods production. This is because the effect of lengthening the horizon on the XY segment of TT is not for X to approach Y, which remains fixed, but for both points to be moved closer to each other.

Thus, suppose that the objective is maximization of the output of machines at the horizon. Then, shifting the horizon from the second to the third periods would mean that the output mix on $T'T'$ would have to contain some textiles instead of only machines. If it is assumed, as was done earlier, that textiles are relatively labor-intensive, the necessary adjustment on TT would be to produce less machines and more textiles. Further extensions of the horizon would reduce the desirable amount of machine production still further, on TT as well as on $T'T'$. It can readily be seen that, whatever the original length of the horizon, extension by one more period reduces the optimal level of machine production and hence raises that of textiles. Consequently, in each of these periods, the terms of trade will be turned in favor of corn, and both employment and the real wage in industry will rise.

The effect on choice of techniques in each sector of industry can also be determined, although with a little more difficulty. The movement along TT in the direction of more textiles and less machines corresponds to a similar movement along the efficiency-locus of the box diagram from which TT is derived. Since textiles are the labor-intensive good, it follows that the capital-labor ratio will be raised in both sectors. Thus the effect on choice of technique has been determined for the initial period.

Similar reasoning cannot be applied to $T'T'$ and subsequent transformation curves since, unlike TT, each of them is not derived from a single box diagram. As textiles are substituted for machines along any one of these curves, however, the "as if" competitively imputed factor cost of a unit of textiles will rise in terms of machines just as along TT, provided that these curves are convex. The convexity of $T'T'$ can be shown to follow from that of FF, which has already been shown to be a consequence of the convexity of *TT* and *OO*. The convexity of the transformation curves for subsequent periods is likewise implied by the convexity of *T'T'*, *OO'*, *OW'* and *F'F'*.

The use of the diagram employed by Lerner (1952, p. 9, Fig. 4) in his proof of the factor-price equalization theorem will indicate that, independently of the change in factor endowments, a rise in the cost of textiles relative to machines will raise the capital-labor ratio in both sectors if textiles is the labor-intensive good. Thus the effect on the choice of techniques in the subsequent periods will be in the same direction as for the initial period.

If the target at the horizon were maximization of the output of textiles the effects on all the variables of extending the horizon by one period would be in the opposite direction to those determined above for the case in which machines are maximized at the horizon. The farther in the future the time at which it is desired to maximize textiles output, the greater in each of the preceding periods will be the optimal amount of machines that have to be produced.

Taken together these results show how the longer the horizon adopted for planning the closer together come the permissible extremes in emphasizing machines or textiles in the intervening periods. In the context of a model with "productive consumption," which is to say a model in which workers and peasants are not physically coerced, the blind application of the "law of superiority of heavy industry to light industry" can be counterproductive, even on its own terms. This is perhaps the most important difference between the implications of the models presented in this and the preceding chapters on the one hand and the widely influential Feldman-Domar-Mahalanobis type of model on the other. Our results will be extended to cover the introduction of foreign trade in chapter 6.

Part Two

THE OPEN DUAL ECONOMY
Growth, The Terms of Trade and the Real Exchange Rate

CHAPTER 4

Growth Maximization and the Internal and External Terms of Trade

IN PART TWO we shall introduce international trade into the formal analysis of the dual economy, as undertaken in Part One for the entirely closed situation. There are a host of important and difficult problems connected with the interrelations of trade and development and we shall certainly not be able to present any single general model that will embrace all, or even perhaps any large, subsets of them. What we shall attempt is the formulation and analysis of three significant aspects of the problem of how foreign trade influences the determination of a dual economy's rate of development. Each aspect will be the concern of one of the chapters. In each chapter the nature of the assumptions about the international trading environment facing the country and the structural specification of the dual economy itself will differ. It is hoped that taken together these chapters will be of some help in illuminating the complexities of the trade-growth nexus.

In this chapter it will be assumed that the only output produced by the modern sector is a single homogeneous industrial commodity that can be used either for consumption or investment. We shall also assume a fixed real wage in terms of food. Both the industrial good and food have fixed prices on the world market, which determine the "external" terms of trade exogenously. Food can also be obtained by trade with the traditional sector, over which the modern sector can exercise monopoly power by preventing free access to the world market through commercial policy or direct state trading. The modern sector can expand food supply through social overhead investment in such projects as irrigation works for which it receives no direct return but which will lower the price of food in terms of the industrial product.

If the objective of the modern sector is taken as a maximization of the rate of growth of its own output, what is the optimal "internal" terms of trade it should set for trade with the traditional sector? In particular should it, and if so to what extent, "exploit" the traditional sector by giving it less favorable terms of trade than those which prevail on the world market? This is the main question to be examined here, together with some related issues on wages and choice of technique.

The problem was first posed and solved by Hornby (1968). We shall, however, give a very simple geometric solution in place of his rather involved mathematics and also correct what appear to be some misinterpretations of the economic meaning that he attaches to his formally correct derivations. In addition the analysis is systematically related to that of Part One of this book and to a contribution by Dixit (1969).[1]

In this chapter the modern sector will continue to be identified with industry and the traditional with agriculture.

I

The industrial sector of the dual economy produces a single homogeneous output that can be used for investment in the industrial sector or as a consumer good by workers and peasants in the agricultural sector. It can also be used for investment in the agricultural sector in the form of social overhead capital, for which no charge is made to the peasants. Industrial output is produced according to a neoclassical constant-returns-to-scale production function with continuous substitution possible between the two

---

[1]See also Bardhan (1970) ch. 9.

inputs, labor and capital (which is the services of the accumulated stock of industrial output not consumed or invested in the agricultural sector). Depreciation is ignored.

The agricultural sector also produces a single homogeneous output, food, which it either consumes or sells to the industrial sector in exchange for manufactured consumer goods. Output in the agricultural sector is proportional to the stock of capital in that sector. Labor is not a scarce factor in this sector; the hours worked are determined by the level of capital. The assumptions necessary for this situation to prevail have been made in chapter 3 and will not be repeated here.

Labor supply to the industrial sector is perfectly elastic at a constant real wage in terms of food. To obtain food the industrial sector must part with some of its output in the form of wages, how much depending upon the volume of employment and the relative price of food and industrial goods. The preferences of workers and peasants for food and manufactured consumer goods are given and are identical for both classes; they are further restricted to a "homothetic" pattern so that the proportion spent on each good is a function only of the relative price ratio and is independent of the level of income.

Decision making in the industrial sector is assumed to be under the control of a state planning agency whose objective is to maximize the growth of the industrial sector. Relations with the agricultural sector are thus only a means to that end. The agricultural sector is beyond the direct control of the planning agency. Direct taxation, for example, is not possible. In Figure 4.1 let *OA* measure the initial capital stock in the industrial sector in terms of the proportionate flow of capital services it makes available. If one also takes the initial labor input as given, the production function of the industrial sector determines the initial level of industrial output. We shall now consider the optimal disposition of this given level of industrial production, between investment in each of the two sectors and wages of the industrial labor force for the next period. If the entire output is devoted to industrial investment, then the industrial capital stock would increase from *OA* to *OB*. Keeping investment in the agricultural sector at zero for the

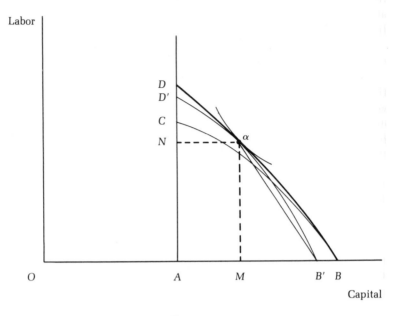

Figure 4.1

moment, we shall determine the possibilities for transforming capital into labor in the industrial sector. If industrial investment is at its maximum, no labor could be hired, since the entire current output would be used up. Real income in the agricultural sector is fixed by the given capital stock in that sector, assuming that capital, once in place, cannot be shifted from one sector to the other. Given any price ratio between food and industrial consumer goods, the consumption preferences of the peasants will then determine how much food they would be willing to exchange with the industrial sector; and this, with a fixed real wage in terms of food, determines how much labor the industrial sector can hire. If units are chosen such that the real wage is one unit of food per unit of labor, then the curve *BC* in Figure 4.1 can be viewed as both an offer curve of the agricultural sector and a factor transformation curve for the industrial sector. At *C* industrial capital is constant but *AC* units of labor would be obtained. The industrial sector could thus obtain any factor combination on the curve *BC*.

The opportunities open to the industrial sector, however, are not confined to the curve *BC*, which corresponds to the case of zero agricultural investment. If some output is used to increase agricultural capital, this will increase the real income of the peasants and so increase the demand for manufactured consumer goods and hence the supply of food at every price ratio. In other words, the offer curve would shift outward. The origin of the offer curve in Figure 4.1 could not remain at *B*, however, since some industrial output has been invested in agriculture. The origin of the offer curve would shift to the left and it would intersect the original curve from below. For each level of agricultural investment there is a particular offer curve. The origin shifts to the left as more output is allocated to increase the stock of agricultural capital. The envelope of all these curves is the solid curve *BD*. The envelope curve *BD* gives the true factor transformation frontier for the industrial sector.

II

In order to find the optimum point on *BD*, we have only to draw the isoquant map for industrial production in Figure 4.1. The tangency point α between *BD* and the highest attainable isoquant determines the optimal disposition of resources in the industrial sector. The optimum capital input into industrial production is *OM*, of which *AM* comes from new investment and the optimum labor input is *AN*. The particular factor transformation curve selected is *B'D'*, which touches the envelope *BD* at α. The optimum investment in the agricultural sector is therefore *BB'*. The distance *MB'* therefore indicates the amount of potential capital services given up in order to obtain *AN* amount of labor and the slope of the line *B'*α determines the optimum terms of trade between food and industrial output. The dimensions of this slope are labor services per unit of capital services, but the price of labor services in terms of food is fixed by the given real wage in terms of food; and since the flow of services from a unit of industrial output serving as a capital good is also fixed, the terms of trade between food and industrial output is strictly determined by the slope of $B'\alpha$. This slope also determines the real wage in terms of industrial output.

The marginal rate of substitution between capital and labor, which determines the choice of technique, is equal not to the slope of $B'\alpha$ but to that of the tangent to the isoquant touching $B'D'$ (and hence BD) at α. This slope represents the marginal rate of transformation between capital and labor. The optimum point α can therefore be characterized by the Dorfman-Samuelson-Solow efficiency condition (familiar from the previous chapter): the marginal rate of transformation between variables considered as the outputs of one period must be equal to the marginal rate of substitution between these same variables when used as inputs in the next period. The monopoly power of the planning agency as a seller of industrial output to the agricultural sector thus leads to a discrepancy between the average and marginal cost of labor when that cost is reckoned in terms of industrial goods. Consequently the industrial sector will equate marginal product not to the real wage itself but to the marginal real cost of labor.

The relation between the wage and the marginal cost of labor, which is the appropriate shadow price, can be expressed in terms of the elasticity of the factor transformation curve $B'D'$, which, it will be recalled, is also the offer curve of the agricultural sector, indicating the terms on which it is prepared to exchange food for manufactures from the industrial sector. Denoting this elasticity by E, the wage by Wa, and the marginal cost of labor by Wm we have

$$E = \frac{Wm}{Wa} \quad \text{or} \quad Wm = E \cdot Wa$$

and from the relation

$$E = \frac{1+e}{e}$$

where e is the ordinary price elasticity of the supply of food we get

$$Wm = \left[1 + \frac{1}{e}\right] Wa$$

which shows that Wm and Wa would be equal only if the elasticity of supply of food were infinite.

As one familiar with the theory of international trade will quickly recognize, this situation is exactly analogous to the "optimum tariff" problem. Here the factor transformation curve $B'D'$ corresponds to the foreign offer curve, and the proportionate difference between Wm and Wa is the tariff We can write the relation as

$$t = \frac{Wm - Wa}{Wa} = \frac{1}{e}$$

and again it may be noted that an infinitely elastic supply results in a zero optimum tariff or no difference between the shadow wage rate and the actual one.

Just as free trade is not optimal for a nation with some monopoly power, it can readily be seen that neither a competitive capitalist regime nor a decentralized socialist one in the industrial sector of a dual economy could achieve the optimal solution in the absence of intervention. Suppose that the optimum amount of agricultural investment BB' is already undertaken, so that AB' is left to be allocated by private capitalists or socialist managers acting on their own. Then the factor proportions chosen at each wage rate can be shown by the locus of points along the "home offer curve" $B'G$ in Figure 4.2 at each of which an isoquant is tangential to a ray from B', representing a fixed wage rate. $B'G$ intersects $B'D'$ at β, resulting in less favorable terms of trade for the industrial sector and less than the maximum attainable rate of growth of industrial output which, as was shown, is secured at the point α on $B'D'$. Employment in the industrial sector will be greater at β than at α.

III

International trade can now be introduced into the model. Initially it will be assumed that the country can export or import food and industrial goods at fixed prices on the world market so that the international terms of trade are given exogenously. As

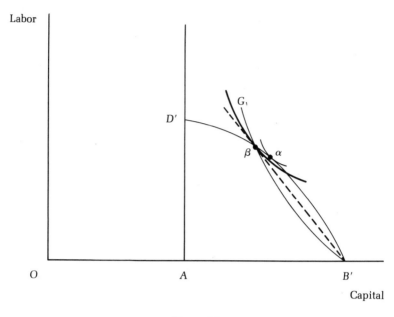

Figure 4.2

explained earlier, units of food can be translated into the labor services that they can command at the fixed wage rate and units of
industrial goods into the flow of capital services they can yield if
used as capital goods. Hence the fixed international terms of trade
imply a fixed rate at which the industrial sector can transform
capital into labor through international trade. The domestic opportunities for effecting this transformation, by means of transac-
tions with the agricultural sector, are of course expressed by the
curve BD in Figure 4.1, which is reproduced in Figure 4.3. The
slope of the line CE, tangent to BD at λ, indicates the rate of transformation of capital into labor attainable through international
trade, derived from the given external terms of trade between food
and industrial goods.

Industrial output, and hence growth (since the initial output
level is given), is maximized at the choice of factor proportions
given by the point λ' on CE where an isoquant is tangential to CE.
These factor proportions are attained in two steps. First, the industrial sector moves from the point B on the horizontal axis to λ,

which is the point at which CE is tangential to BD by investing BB' in the agricultural sector and then trading industrial goods equivalent to $B'M$ of capital for food equivalent to AN of labor with the domestic agricultural sector. It then exports food equivalent to NN' of labor to the outside world in exchange for imports of industrial goods equivalent to MM' of capital. Of course if the tangency point λ' were to the left of λ there would be export of industrial goods and import of food.

It can be seen that efficiency requires the marginal rate of transformation of capital into labor, and hence of industrial goods into food, to be the same in both domestic and international trade. Internationally, the marginal and average rates of transformation are the same, but domestically the marginal cost of food will be higher than the average cost, since the average cost is rising at the point λ. The industrial sector therefore "exploits" the agricultural sector by giving it less favorable terms of trade, measured by the slope of $B'\lambda$, for its food exports than it receives itself from the rest of the world by reexporting some of the food that it obtains from the domestic agricultural sector. This result can be achieved either by a state monopoly of export trade or by free markets combined with an export tax on food that cuts the internal terms of trade for the peasants by the appropriate amount. This form of "primitive socialist accumulation" has long been practiced by the Burmese rice export agency, for example.

If λ' were to the left of λ then the industrial sector would have to increase the supply of food further by importing it from the rest of the world in return for industrial exports. Again, there will be a gap between the internal and external terms of trade, with the industrial sector equalizing cost at the margin but paying a lower average price to the domestic agricultural sector than it has to pay to the rest of the world.

The presence of some monopoly power in international as well as internal trade can also be allowed for by using the "Baldwin Envelope" technique. The foreign offer curve can be made to slide along the domestic factor transformation envelope BD and the locus of points at which domestic and foreign marginal rates of transformation are equated can be traced out. The result is that the

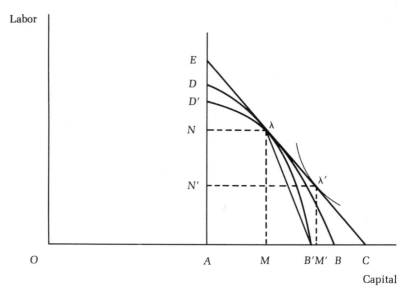

Figure 4.3

line CE in Figure 4.3, which is the boundary of the possibility set in the fixed terms of trade case, will be drawn in at the ends so that it becomes a curve concave to the origin. Optimal investment and trade policies can be derived as before. Since both domestic and foreign rates of transformation are equated at the margin, the relationship between the internal and external terms of trade will be determined by the relative elasticities at the optimal points of the offer curves of the domestic agricultural sector and the rest of the world. The industrial sector is thus in the position of a discriminating monopolist.

The apparently surprising need for the price ratio to domestic producers to diverge from the international price ratio, when the latter is fixed exogenously, may be worth some further discussion and analysis. Using Figure 4.4, suppose that domestic producers are offered the same price ratio that prevails externally. The supply of food in labor equivalents and the demand for industrial goods in capital equivalents would be determined by the point c on $B'D'$ where it is intersected by a line from B', the slope of

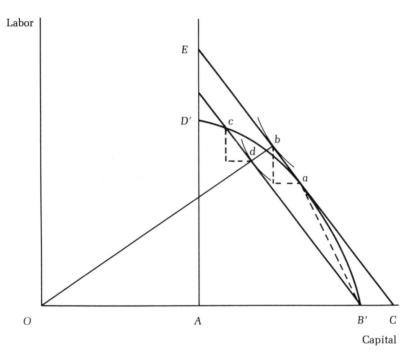

Figure 4.4

which measures the international terms of trade in labor-capital
equivalents. Maximization of industrial growth will occur at the
point d, where an isoquant is tangential to the international terms
of trade line originating at B'. This involves export of food and import of industrial goods. It can clearly be seen, however, that this
solution is inferior to that of selecting the point a on B'D' by restricting the internal terms of trade for the agricultural sector to
the slope of B'a, and then exporting industrial goods and importing food so as to move to the point b, which represents greater industrial growth than the point d. The reason for this is that the additional domestic supply of food at c as compared with a on B'D'
is obtained at a marginal cost higher than the international price
ratio. The case for the divergence of the domestic price ratio is
thus simply the familiar rule that marginal cost and not average
cost should be equalized when there are two sources of supply.

IV

We have so far limited our discussion to a single period. However, we shall now investigate the characteristics of the time path of the solution. It can be readily seen that the nature of the time path is balanced growth at the maximal rate, or growth on the "von Neumann path." To demonstrate this we may simply note that all functions represented in Figure 4.1 are homogeneous of degree one. As time passes all magnitudes simply increase in the same proportion and the structural properties of the solution remain unchanged. The industrial and agricultural production functions are of constant returns to scale by assumption and the factor transformation curves are homogeneous of degree one because the preferences of the agricultural sector between food and industrial goods are assumed to have this property. At any price ratio the amount of labor services obtainable in exchange for the surrender of potential capital services is determined by the proportion of food exchanged for industrial goods by the peasants. This by hypothesis is independent of their income level.

The problem can be approached as one of obtaining the maximum steady rate of return on the fixed initial level of industrial output, considered as an investment by the industrial sector itself. This investment has to be optimally allocated among three uses—fixed capital formation in the industrial and agricultural sectors respectively, and "working capital" in the form of a "wage fund" in terms of food obtained by trade with the agricultural sector (and also the outside world if international trade is possible). The necessary conditions for achieving this optimal disposition have been worked out for the first period and the solution for all subsequent periods follows from the fact that the maximized output of each period becomes the input for the next. Industrial and agricultural output grow at the same rate as does the marketed surplus. The factor proportions in industry and the terms of trade between the two sectors of the dual economy remain constant over time. The introduction of international trade leads to a permanent once-over increase in the maximum growth rate attainable.

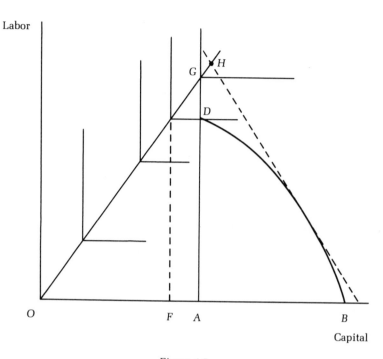

Figure 4.5

The von Neumann path of balanced growth at the maximum rate may not be immediately attainable if there is an initial imbalance in the relative quantities of agricultural and industrial capital. This situation is most clearly apparent if we assume, as in Figure 4.5, fixed coefficients for the industrial production function. In the case depicted, industrial technology is sufficiently labor-intensive for the ray through the origin connecting the corners of the L-shaped isoquants to intersect the perpendicular at A above the point D, where it is met by the factor transformation envelope BD. It is thus impossible for the existing industrial capital stock to be fully utilized. Output is maximized with labor input at the limit of AD and capital input of OF, which means that FA of industrial capital is redundant. All new investment of course is directed to agriculture. The factor transformation curve shifts outward and eventually the excess industrial capacity would be eliminated and the von Neumann path followed thereafter.

It is interesting to note that in the "corner solution" just discussed growth maximization implies employment maximization in the industrial sector, whereas in the case of an interior solution there is a conflict between the two. In Figure 4.1, the growth rate of industrial output is maximized at α whereas industrial employment and agricultural investment and output are maximized at the terminal point D on the factor transformation envelope BD. Thus from B to α on BD, employment and output are both rising in the industrial sector, whereas from α to D employment continues to rise but output falls, as the additional employment does not compensate sufficiently for the potential capital services sacrificed. Selection of a point on BD to the left of α could still yield balanced growth, but not at the maximum rate. Employment would initially be higher, but given sufficient time the von Neumann path would eventually yield a higher absolute level of employment also, since the rate of growth of employment is greatest on that path.

The possibility of international trade can remove the necessity for a corner solution. In Figure 4.5 let the dashed line tangential to BD (denoting international trade opportunities at fixed prices) meet the vertical axis above the point G (which is the level of employment required for full utilization of the existing industrial capital stock). The optimal solution is now an interior balanced growth one at H, with a positive new investment in the industrial sector. International trade has created a "vent" for the previously redundant industrial capital by providing cheaper food, thus making it possible to increase industrial employment. It is of course possible that the point G would not be attainable even with international trade if the terms of trade are not sufficiently favorable. International trade would then reduce excess industrial capacity, but not eliminate it entirely.

V

In this final section of the chapter, we shall make some notes and comments on the literature concerning the problems discussed here. This should be of some use, particularly as the various contributions have never been systematically related to each other. The model we have analyzed in this chapter is essentially a graphic version of the model presented by Hornby, which we hope has helped to simplify and clarify the underlying economic logic of his elaborate mathematical derivations. Hornby also made no attempt to relate his model to any previous work on the subject, apparently believing it to be nonexistent.

As we have seen, the basic optimality condition of the model can be interpreted as the Dorfman-Samuelson-Solow intertemporal efficiency condition of equality between marginal rates of transformation and substitution. In chapter 3, which is based on Findlay (1962), we have explicitly adopted a Dorfman-Samuelson-Solow type of approach to the problem of development in a dual economy. Factor transformation curves for each period analogous to the construction used here were derived, and the result obtained demonstrated that the intertemporally efficient segment of these curves was an intermediate segment that became increasingly narrower as the finite horizon was moved farther into the future. In the present analysis this segment collapses into a single point. The reason for this difference is that the model of chapter 3 distinguishes capital goods and consumer goods in the output of the industrial sector whereas here it is assumed that industrial production is physically homogeneous. In this respect, therefore, the Hornby model is a special case of the earlier model. Hornby, however, did make two important extensions of the analysis: the inclusion of unrequited investment by the industrial sector in the agricultural sector, and the possibility of international trade.

Dixit's model differs from Hornby's in that it assumes fixed coefficients for the industrial production function and in the objective of the planners, which is taken to be the attainment of a prescribed industrial capital stock in minimum time. This enables the powerful methods of Pontryagin's "maximum principle" to be applied. However, if the capital stock target is large enough to require a "long" period of time to reach it, the solution path follows the von Neumann path except at the beginning and the end. The possibility that a "corner solution" will occur because the industrial and agricultural capital stocks are not in the required balance has been analyzed in the present chapter, and it is this which gives rise to the unbalanced phases of the Dixit solution. He also allows for the possibility that peasants and workers may have different tastes, one consequence of which is that the state could make some additional profit by "buying cheap" from peasants and "selling dear" to workers. He incorrectly states, however, that if tastes are uniform the optimum solution is attainable by free competition. As we have seen, there has to be some monopolistic restriction improving the industrial terms of trade for the optimal solution to be attained.

It was noted earlier that the marginal product of labor in industry must be equated not to the real wage in terms of industrial goods, but to the marginal real cost of labor in terms of those goods. Hornby states that this divergence is the same result as that obtained by Eckstein (1957), Sen (1960), and Marglin (1967) in their writings on the choice of technique problem for the industrial sector of a dual economy. All these writers, however, assumed the terms of trade to be fixed in their models and the divergence they obtain between the marginal product and the real wage is due to the attachment of some weight to consumption in the present instead of following a purely growth-maximizing strategy. Employment and consumption in the present are therefore greater than they would be if growth maximization were the objective. Hornby, however, assumes growth maximization and still gets a divergence, unlike the Eckstein-Sen-Marglin case. The reason is that the terms of trade are variable and marginal cost of labor exceeds average cost in his model. The divergence is in the opposite direction, with employment being *less* than what it would be if marginal product were equated to the wage.

Hornby's apparent misinterpretation of his results is perhaps due to his tendency to oppose his own "dynamic" analysis to conventional static analysis and to attribute any difference in conclusions reached to this factor. However, as we have seen, the cause of the wage's divergence from the marginal product of labor was not any "dynamic" element but simply the assumption of some degree of monopoly power by the planned industrial sector over the atomistic peasant sector. Another important example in the same vein is Hornby's statement that the efficient trade policy in his model contradicts the principle of comparative advantage. The industrial sector would export industrial goods and import food if the international price of food were lower than the marginal cost of food in isolation. The price of food in isolation, however, would be lower than the marginal cost in isolation; and it might be lower than the international price when the opportunity to trade arises. Hornby sees this as a contradiction of comparative advantage, since food is imported even though its internal price is lower, and again attributes the difference to "dynamics." All contradiction disappears, however, when it is realized that the relevant comparison is always between international and domestic marginal cost. Prices can be compared to infer comparative advantage only if there is perfect competition internally and externally, which is not the case in the present instance as a result of the industrial sector's monopoly power over the domestic agricultural sector.

Finally, it should be realized that the divergence of the internal from the external terms of trade is optimal only because it is assumed that the planners are unable to impose direct taxation on the agricultural sector to the extent required by a policy of maximum growth. If it is assumed that they have this power, the best policy would be to allow the exogenously determined price ratio to prevail in the domestic agricultural sector; this policy would encourage food production until marginal cost to *peasants* were equated to the world price, with direct land taxes imposed at the level appropriate for siphoning off the necessary surplus to finance industrial growth at the maximum rate. The exercise of a monopolistic price policy with the local agricultural sector getting less than the world price for food is justifiable only as a "second best" optimal strategy. The situation is analogous to the Galenson-Leibenstein (1955) argument for maximizing profit rather than output when the opportunity cost of labor is below the real wage that has to be paid, since savings are a function of profits rather than income.

In any policy recommendations, therefore, the widespread

practice in some less developed countries of using price policies toward the agricultural sector that reduce the incentive to expand output have to be examined carefully, and should only be followed if it is in fact difficult to rely on direct taxation to the extent needed. In any case the argument given here shows that a policy of twisting the terms of trade too adversely against the peasants can be self-defeating for the industrial sector, a truth that Stalin's victim Bukharin perceived a long time ago during the famous "scissors crisis" of the Soviet Union in the 1920s.

To take a more recent historical example, the Burmese rice marketing board's policy of severely depressing the price to cultivators must clearly have exceeded any theoretically defensible optimum—as can be seen by the sharp decline in both the absolute level of rice exports and the share of the market in comparison with Thailand. Ideological prejudices and administrative difficulties prevented reliance on direct land taxation, the mainstay of colonial finances, as a superior instrument for the extraction of the agricultural surplus.

CHAPTER 5

Primary Exports, Manufacturing Production, and the Rate of Growth

FEW THEMES have been more repeatedly stressed in the vast literature on economic development than the slow growth of world demand for primary exports, which inhibits the growth prospects of the Third World. This notion lies at the core of the Prebisch thesis of secular deterioration in the terms of trade of the developing countries, the more recent "foreign exchange gap" theory, and the Nurkse "balanced growth" doctrine, which he recommended as a substitute for the nineteenth-century pattern of trade-propelled growth.

In view of this it is surprising that the rate of growth of world demand for a developing country's primary exports seldom appears explicitly in formal models of economic development. One exception is Seers (1962), in which a very simple model is constructed to show the dependence of growth in the "periphery" of the world economy on the rate at which it takes place in the "center." Writing Yc, Yp for real income levels in the two areas and Mc, Mp for import levels we have, assuming linear functional relationships between imports and income and balanced trade, the relation

$$Yp = \frac{(A - a) + BYc}{b}$$

derived from equating $Mc = A + BYc$ and $Mp = a + bYp$.

If growth at the center is independently determined at a rate r so that $Yc(t) = \bar{Y}ce^{rt}$ while growth at the periphery is purely dependent the relative income levels can be written.

$$\frac{Yp}{Yc} = \frac{B}{b} + \frac{(A-a)}{b\bar{Y}ce^{rt}}$$

from which it follows that if A is greater than a income at the periphery relative to income at the center will decline asymptotically, which is the familiar story of the "widening gap."

This model is much too crude and rigid to be acceptable. Relative prices are ignored, structural change can find no place, and such questions as why the periphery cannot raise its growth by increased saving or technical progress can find no answer within this framework. It is true that Seers discusses all these and other problems very cogently in his paper, but he does not succeed in integrating them into the model itself.

A more interesting model is presented in the fourth chapter of the recent book by Bardhan (1970). The developing country produces, under conditions represented by a Cobb-Douglas function, a single output by means of labor, capital, and an imported intermediate input, which cannot be produced domestically and without which no output is possible. World demand for the country's product is price inelastic and grows at a fixed rate, as does labor, while the growth of capital is governed by a proportional saving function. Trade is always balanced. Bardhan shows that the steady-state growth rate of capital will be a weighted average of the growth rates of labor and world demand for exports. Hence if the latter is smaller than the former, which he says is likely to be the case for India and most developing countries other than the oil exporters, the growth rate of domestic output will be lower than that of labor and per capita output will be falling. Since he shows that the terms of trade will also be declining, per capita income must be falling continuously over time—a very pessimistic conclusion indeed.

The assumption of a single type of output for which world demand is sluggish prevents structural change in the Bardhan model also, and while the assumption of slow growth in demand for most types of primary commodities may be justified, there is always the possibility of developing manufactured exports, for which the small share of the market that any particular developing country could have means that demand would be highly, if not perfectly, elastic. While there have been a number of descriptive and empirical studies of manufactured exports from the developing counties, notably by Lary (1968) there does not appear to have been any formal model incorporating this feature.

This chapter will combine the slow growth of demand for primary exports with the possibility of developing manufactured exports in a model of dual economy development in which there is no domestic capital goods production. The chapter's main concern will be the conditions determining whether the developing dual economy can attain a growth rate permanently higher than the rate at which world demand for the primary exportable is expanding.

I

It will initially be assumed that the sole output produced by the modern sector consists of an exportable primary product for which there is no domestic demand at all, for either consumption or investment. One readily thinks of Malayan rubber, Chilean copper, and Ghanaian cocoa in this connection, although of course there are cases such as Argentine beef or Burmese rice, for which this assumption is not valid. A neoclassical production function, with constant returns to scale and variable input proportions—the inputs being labor and malleable capital—is assumed to describe the technology for producing this primary exportable. The initial stock of capital is taken as given. Labor is in perfectly elastic supply from the traditional sector at a fixed real wage in terms of manufactured consumer goods, which can be exchanged as desired with the traditional sector (or the rest of the world) for food at a fixed ratio.

The country is assumed to be too small to affect the prices of manufactured consumer goods and capital goods on the world market, which will be taken as constant throughout the analysis. When it comes to the market for the primary exportable, however, the country is able to influence the price, so that there is a downward sloping demand curve for exports which moves to the right at the same constant rate at each price. For convenience, units should be chosen so that one unit of manufactured consumer goods has the same value as one unit of capital goods (since the prices of these are assumed fixed) and to measure the price of the exportable relative to this common unit.

Output and employment in the modern sector, and the relative price of the primary exportable, are determined on the assumption that profits are maximized. Account is taken of the degree of monopoly that can be exercised on the world market. This result can be achieved by monopolistic private enterprise, by competitive private enterprise with an appropriate national trade policy, or directly by state enterprise.

Equilibrium price, output, and employment at any moment can conveniently be depicted by the familiar diagram of Figure 5.1. The average and marginal revenue curves are not restricted to any particular form at this stage of the discussion. The marginal cost curve is upward sloping because there are diminishing returns to successive increments of labor applied to a fixed capital stock and because there is a fixed cost per unit of additional labor. Profits are maximized at an output of OQ and a price of OP, with OM measuring the common value of marginal revenue and marginal cost. Employment can be determined from the production function, the fixed initial capital stock, and the equilibrium level of output.

The total value of output in the modern sector is given by the rectangle $OPFQ$. The area $ONEQ$ under the marginal cost curve is the wage bill. The area MNE represents the total rental value of the fixed capital stock when output is valued at marginal revenue OM instead of the actual world price OP. The area $MPFE$ indicates the pure monopoly profit arising out of following the optimally restrictive trade policy, with MP/OP representing the optimum rate of export taxation. The "surplus" income or the difference between the total value of output and the wage bill thus can be

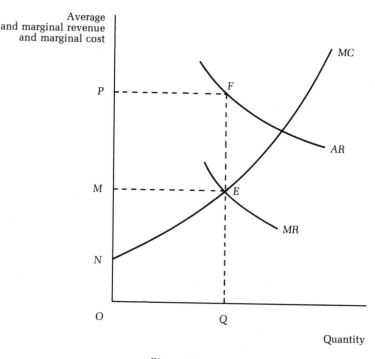

Figure 5.1

broken down, at least conceptually, into two parts, one consisting
of pure monopoly profit and the other the rental income of the
capital stock evaluated at its marginal revenue product.

The uses to which this total income is put can now be examined. On the usual assumption that all wages are spent on consumption there will be imports of manufactured consumer goods
into the country at least equal in amount to the wage bill. If part of
the surplus income is used for additional luxury consumption,
there will be additional imports of manufactured consumer goods.
The rest of the surplus is assumed to be used to import capital
goods. Of course in colonial economies a considerable part of the
surplus would simply be remitted abroad, but this possibility is
excluded here. It then follows that there must be balanced trade,
since the total value of exports—which on the assumptions made
is the total value of output in the modern sector—is spent either

on capital goods or manufactured consumer goods, both of which can be obtained only through importation.

If one writes s for the propensity to save out of profits, Π for total profits, K for the capital stock, and ignores depreciation, it follows that the rate of capital accumulation is

$$\frac{\dot{K}}{K} = s\,\frac{\Pi}{K} \tag{5.1}$$

The accumulation of capital will naturally shift the equilibrium point of Figure 5.1. The demand curve shifts exogenously to the right at the same rate for each price, and independently of the rate of capital accumulation. If the demand curve is restricted so that it has a constant price elasticity at all points, it follows that the marginal revenue curve will also shift to the right at the same rate, since marginal revenue is equal to $(1 - 1/\eta)$ times the price where η is the price elasticity of demand, so that the same price always corresponds to the same marginal revenue. The marginal cost curve, however, does depend on the rate of capital accumulation, and the extent to which it shifts has now to be determined.

It is readily apparent that the marginal cost of the primary exportable is equal to the real wage rate in terms of the manufactured consumer goods divided by the marginal physical productivity of labor in producing the primary exportable. The real wage is fixed by assumption, and this means that the ratio of capital to labor—and hence the marginal product of labor as well—will also be constant at a fixed price ratio. But capital has increased at the rate described in (5.1), so employment and hence output also must have increased in the same proportion. It has thus been shown that for each value of marginal cost the curve is shifted to the right at the same rate at which capital is growing.

Suppose that the rate at which capital grows is higher than the exogenous rate λ at which world demand increases. It would then follow that, at the equilibrium level OM of marginal cost and marginal revenue, output exceeds the demand at the original price (by the assumption of constant elasticity). The price must fall, since the new marginal revenue and marginal costs curves intersect below OM. The lower equilibrium value of marginal cost implies that the marginal physical product of labor must have risen, since the real wage in terms of manufactures is fixed. Employment, and hence output, must therefore grow more slowly than capital if capital is growing at a rate greater than λ.

The rate of growth of capital, as shown by (5.1), depends on the rate of profit in the modern sector, which will itself be affected by what happens to employment, output, and price. The rate of profit, or the ratio of total profits to the stock of capital, can be written, recalling the earlier discussion of its two components, as

$$\frac{\Pi}{K} = \frac{\dfrac{\partial C}{\partial Q}\dfrac{\partial Q}{\partial K}K + \dfrac{1}{\eta}pQ}{K} = \frac{\partial C}{\partial Q}\frac{\partial Q}{\partial K} + \frac{p}{\eta}\frac{Q}{K} \qquad (5.2)$$

where $\partial C/\partial Q$ is the marginal cost of the exportable in terms of manufactures, $\partial Q/\partial K$ is the marginal physical product of capital, p is the price of the exportable in terms of manufactures, and Q is the physical output of the exportable. The first term in the numerator is therefore the rental value of the capital stock evaluated at the margin. The second term is the pure monopoly profit, defined as the difference between price and marginal revenue times the quantity of exports. The expression given follows from substituting $(1 - 1/\eta)$ times the price for marginal revenue. It should be noted that η has to be greater than unity for the problem to be meaningful, since a constant elasticity demand curve of less than unit elasticity would imply unbounded revenue as output falls, which is absurd.

It has already been shown that $\partial C/\partial Q$ falls and that $\partial Q/\partial K$ must also fall, since employment increases less than the capital stock. It has also been shown that p falls and that Q/K also has to fall, since Q rises more slowly than K. Hence it has been shown that if capital grows at a rate greater than λ, the rate of profit must fall. But this in turn implies that the rate of growth of capital must decline, by the relation depicted in (5.1). It therefore follows that the rate of growth of capital, if initially above λ, must in the long run converge to this value. Similar arguments will show that if initially below λ the rate of growth of capital must rise. Hence the steady-state solution is for capital, employment, and output all to increase at the rate of λ—the rate of growth of world demand —with the rate of profit equal to λ/s.

In a recent article Corden (1971) refers to "supply-motored" and "demand-motored" models of trade and growth. His own contribution concentrates on the former. Discussion of the latter type of model has usually been confined to somewhat loose generalizations and historical descriptions on the theme of "export-led growth," of which the famous "staple" theory is one example. The model discussed in this section is a simple but well defined case of purely dependent growth, in which the "enclave" economy can grow no faster in the limit than whatever rate at which world demand for the exportable happens to be increasing. A higher rate of saving ultimately only lowers the rate of profit, leaving the growth rate of capital and employment unchanged.

II

Before turning to the analysis of both primary and manufacturing production in the modern sector it would perhaps be useful to contrast the pure primary production or "enclave" model of the last section with a pure manufacturing model. The manufactured good produced under constant returns to scale could be considered as being both a consumer as well as a capital good, in which case the model could operate without any international trade, or as a consumer good exchangeable for capital goods on the world market at fixed terms of trade. The analysis would be identical in both cases.

In this model the rate of growth of capital would be

$$\frac{\dot{K}}{K} = s \, \frac{\Pi}{K} = s \, \frac{\partial M}{\partial K} \, (w) \qquad (5.3)$$

where $\partial M/\partial K$ is the marginal product of capital in the production of manufactures and w is the real wage rate. Since s and w are constants it follows that the rate of growth of capital is a constant. Profit maximization implies that the marginal product of labor is

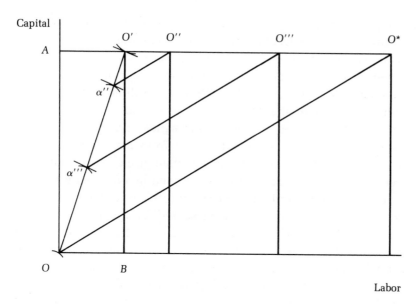

Figure 5.2

always equated to the constant real wage, which means that the rate of growth of employment must be equal to that of capital, to ensure a constant capital-labor ratio.

In this model the rate of growth varies directly with the propensity to save out of profits and inversely with the real wage rate. This is in sharp contrast to the model of the previous section, where ultimately the sole determinant of the rate of growth was the growth rate of external demand. It would therefore be of some interest to examine the relative strength of these alternative determinants in a model that combines both primary and manufacturing production in the modern sector.

Given the wage rate and the initial capital stock, the maximum level of manufacturing output consistent with profit maximization can readily be determined by the condition that employment is carried to the point at which marginal labor productivity in manufacturing is equal to the wage rate. This is depicted in Figure 5.2, in which the given capital stock OA is shown combined with OB of labor to produce the level of output corresponding to the isoquant on which the equilibrium point O' is situated. The capital-labor ratio OA/OB used in the production of manufactures is determined by the given wage rate.

Suppose we now desire to produce some primary output, again in a manner consistent with profit maximization. If the usual assumption is made that there cannot be any output without some input of capital, then the only way in which some primary output can be produced is to divert capital from manufacturing. The capital-labor ratio OA/OB in manufacturing must, however, remain unchanged, since it is determined by the fixed wage rate and profit maximization. The opportunity cost of labor and capital in primary production is measured by the real wage and marginal product of capital in manufactures, the former fixed by assumption and the latter determined uniquely as a consequence. Thus relative factor prices and hence the capital-labor ratio in primary production are also uniquely determined by conditions in the manufacturing subsector.

If it is assumed that manufacturing is capital-intensive as compared to primary production, total employment will increase as capital is switched from manufacturing to primary production, with the capital-labor ratio unchanged in each subsector. This is shown by the extended labor axis of the successive "boxes" in Figure 5.2, with primary output measured from the origins O'', O''', etc. The lengths of the parallel vectors from these origins to the points α'', α''', etc., at which they intersect OO', are proportional to the output levels of the primary good, while the distance along OO' from O to the intersection point indicates the corresponding level of manufacturing output in each case. Employment increases as the origin for the primary goods isoquant family is shifted to the right, until at O^* the entire capital stock is allocated to the primary sector. The slopes of the vectors OO' and OO^* mark the two limiting extremes for the overall ratio of labor to capital in the modern sector as a whole.

Each of the successive boxes defines a transformation curve between manufacturing and primary output. Each curve lies successively outside its predecessor, since capital is fixed and employ-

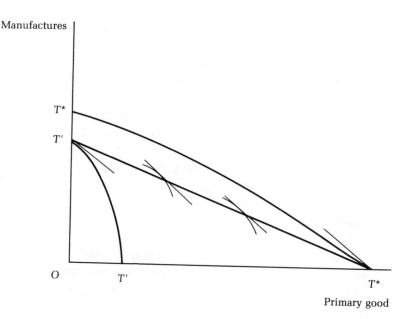

Figure 5.3

ment is increasing. These curves are shown in Figure 5.3, with $T'T'$ corresponding to factor proportions OO' and T^*T^* to OO^*. However, the fact that the real wage rate and hence relative factor prices are given exogenously implies that production will take place on each curve only at one point: that at which the given relative factor prices prevail. In terms of Figure 5.2, these points will correspond to O and O' at the extremes and α'', α''', etc. in between. By the well-known correspondence between factor and commodity price ratios this means that relative commodity prices or the slopes of the transformation curves at the production points will be constant. At this price ratio the curve $T'T'$ will indicate complete specialization on manufactures and the curve T^*T^* complete specialization on the primary good. All intermediate points will lie on the "Rybczynski line" $T'T^*$, which is the locus of all the successive production points that have their slopes determined by the given factor-price ratio.

The linearity of the Rybczynski locus can readily be proved by Figure 5.2, when one recalls that the lengths of vectors from the origins measure output levels and uses the properties of similar triangles to show that the ratio of the increment in primary output to the reduction in manufacturing output remains constant as employment is increased. The economic reason for the linearity is also clear: capital is being switched from one branch to the other with the capital-output ratio in both sectors remaining constant, and employment is being adjusted appropriately. The slope of the Rybczynski line is therefore equal to the quotient of the two constant capital-output ratios.

Since the Rybczynski line $T'T^*$ in some way corresponds to the transformation curve of an economic system with employment variable, fixed capital stock, and exogenously determined factor prices, it might be thought that its slope determines the marginal cost of the primary good in terms of manufactures. However this is not true, since employment is increasing as primary output is substituted for manufacturing, and this additional employment involves a cost. The relationship between the slope of the Rybczynski line and the true marginal cost of the primary good is brought out by means of the Lerner diagram of Figure 5.4.

In this diagram the slopes of OR and OS indicate the capital-labor ratios in manufacturing and primary production respectively. The lengths of OR and OS denote the output levels attainable with one unit of capital. By the argument given earlier, the slope of the Rybczynski line is equal to the quotient of the capital-output ratios which is $\overline{OR}/\overline{OS}$ in this case. But producing $\overline{OS}$ amount of the primary good involves using RS more labor, SU of which—at the given relative factor prices—is worth TU of capital, which makes it possible to raise the output of manufactures to $\overline{OT}$. Thus the marginal cost of the primary good in terms of manufactures is $\overline{OT}/\overline{OS}$, since it is these two magnitudes that have the same resource cost. In terms of Figure 5.3, the marginal cost is measured by the common slope of the transformation curves at each point on the Rybczynski line.

It has therefore been shown that so long as there is any production of manufactures the marginal cost of producing the primary

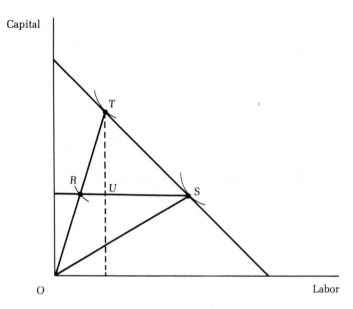

Figure 5.4

good is constant. If production is extended on the horizontal axis of Figure 5.3 beyond T^*, however, then the only way to increase output is by employing more labor on a fixed capital stock, so that diminishing marginal labor productivity with a fixed wage rate means that marginal cost will be rising.

The analysis has so far been conducted on the assumption that manufactures are relatively capital intensive. If the opposite assumption is made, marginal cost under incomplete specialization will still be constant as before. However employment will decline as the primary good's output is increased and the successive transformation curves of Figure 5.3 will lie inside rather than outside their predecessors. The common slope of the transformation curves along the Rybczynski line, equal to the marginal cost of the primary good in terms of manufactures, will be flatter instead of steeper than the Rybczynski line itself. After the point of complete specialization is reached, employment will increase again and marginal cost will rise as before. Employment as a function of the

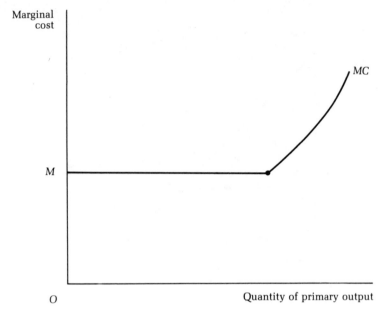

Figure 5.5

level of primary output will therefore follow a U-shaped curve that falls as manufacturing output is reduced to zero and rises thereafter.

Figure 5.5 shows the marginal cost of primary production in terms of manufactures as a function of the level of primary production. The curve has a flat portion corresponding to constant marginal cost under incomplete specialization and a rising portion after all capital has been allocated to primary production and the output of manufactures has fallen to zero.

The price of the primary exportable, the level of both outputs and of employment, and the allocation of the capital stock between the two branches are determined once the demand curve—and hence the marginal revenue curve—is specified. It can be seen that so long as the marginal revenue curve intersects the marginal cost curve on the flat portion, the price of the exportable is independent of demand and is simply determined by the real wage rate and the technology for the two goods. Price varies with demand only when the economy is completely specialized; that is, when the marginal revenue curve intersects the marginal cost curve on its rising portion. In the case of incomplete specialization the output of the primary good is determined from Figure 5.5; this in turn can determine manufacturing output, capital allocation, and employment from Figure 5.2.

Now that the momentary equilibrium of the system has been determined, attention can be turned to the factors governing the rate of growth. It will be convenient to introduce the following notation: g is the rate of growth of capital at any instant; let μ be the rate of growth of capital when there is no production of the primary exportable, so that it is equal to $s \, \partial M/\partial K \, (w)$, the right-hand side of (5.3); λ as defined earlier, is the rate of growth of world demand for the primary exportable at any given price.

Suppose that the initial conditions are such that the marginal revenue curve intersects the marginal cost curve on its rising segment. In this case, it is clear that the marginal revenue product of capital will be higher than what it would be if any capital were allocated to the manufacturing sector. Moreover, there is additional profit because of the excess of price over marginal revenue. The rate of growth of capital must therefore be higher than μ. The value of λ in relation to g and μ determines a set of possible situations, each of which is analyzed below:

1. $g > \lambda > \mu$. It has already been shown that if only the primary good is produced and $g > \lambda$ then the price of the exportable will fall and so will g, since it depends upon the rate of profit. In terms of Figure 5.5, the turning point on the marginal cost curve moves to the right at the rate of g (since output is proportional to capital with a fixed capital-labor ratio) while the marginal revenue curve shifts to the right at the rate of λ. If g converges to λ before the turning point of the marginal cost curve overtakes the marginal revenue curve, the economy would specialize forever in the primary exportable. The introduction of the possibility of manufacturing production makes no difference to the analysis of the model of section I, since it is never profitable to divert any capital to it.

The other possibility is that the price continues to decline until intersection of the two curves takes place on the flat portion of the marginal cost curve, with g still greater than λ. Marginal revenue, price, and marginal cost will all remain constant from then on. The turning point of the marginal cost curve shifts to the right at the rate of g, while the marginal revenue curve moves to the right at the slower rate of λ. This means that a falling proportion of capital is allocated to the primary exportable, since the level of output at which the marginal cost curve turns upward is proportional to the total capital stock, with the capital-labor ratio fixed.

What happens to the rate of profit during this process? The marginal revenue product of capital is equal in both subsectors, since profit is always being maximized at each instant, and is constant over time since the wage rate, technology, and the marginal revenue of the primary exportable in terms of manufactures remain unchanged. Total profit, however, also consists of the pure monopoly profit on primary exports. Since price and marginal revenue remain constant, this monopoly profit is proportional to the output of the primary good, which in turn is proportional to the capital allocated to its production as a result of the capital-labor ratio being unchanged. Writing r for the common marginal revenue product of capital in the two branches, b for the output-capital ratio in primary production, and $\widetilde{K}$ for capital allocated to that branch we have, for the rate of profit

$$\frac{\Pi}{K} = r + \frac{p}{\eta}\, b\, \frac{\widetilde{K}}{K} \tag{5.4}$$

Since it was shown earlier that $\widetilde{K}/K$ is falling if $g > \lambda$, it follows that the rate of profit will be declining. This in turn implies that g must be falling so that eventually in the steady state g will equal λ while a constant fraction of resources will be devoted to each branch so that there will be balanced growth at the rate of λ. Manufactured consumer goods produced internally may be supplemented by imports or may be partly exported, depending upon whether primary exports exceed or fall short of capital good imports.

2. $g > \mu > \lambda$ This case is exactly like the first, insofar as $g > \lambda$, but with the crucial difference that g cannot fall below μ so that

the steady state toward which the system tends is determined by internal instead of external conditions. Since $g > \lambda$ and $\lambda < \mu$ the marginal revenue curve must eventually cut the marginal cost curve on its flat portion. With $g > \lambda$ the turning point of the marginal cost curve shifts to the right faster than the intersection with the marginal revenue curve, so that the proportion of capital allocated to primary production continually declines, although the absolute value of capital in this branch increases at the rate of λ. There is also a continual fall in g, since the rate of profit is declining as shown by (5.4), but the limit is μ not λ. In other words as $\widetilde{K}/K$ falls toward zero the rate of profit eventually tends toward r, which is what it would be if the modern sector produced manufactures alone, with $g = sr$.

The opportunity to engage in primary exports always raises the rate of profit above r, but the failure of external demand to grow faster than sr means that eventually primary exports become increasingly negligible for the economy. Capital goods imports get paid for by exports of manufactured consumer goods, which initially may not even be produced at all.

The economy can thus go through a phase of complete specialization on primary production followed by a phase of progressive import substitution of manufactured consumer goods until finally the stage of exporting these goods is reached. Primary exports continue to increase at the rate of λ, but since the limiting growth rate for the economy is $sr = \mu > \lambda$ their relative importance continually declines.

3. $\lambda > g > \mu$. It can be seen from the logic of the previous cases that under these conditions the rate of profit and hence g will rise until it approaches λ in the steady state. If there is incomplete specialization initially, there may be either complete specialization on the primary product in the steady state or incomplete specialization with a higher proportion of capital devoted to primary production as compared with the initial situation. If there is complete specialization on the primary good to begin with, it will continue. This case was already examined in section I, since manufacturing production possibilities are irrelevant under these circumstances.

In the analysis of this and the preceding section, frequent use has been made of the notion of the rate of growth in the steady state. It should be emphasized, however, that this term can only be used in a rather loose way in the present context, because the dual economy feature of unlimited labor supply at a fixed real wage rate cannot persist forever but is itself only a phase of the total development process. Thus, when it is said that g tends to λ or to μ as a limiting value, it should always be understood that the statement is strictly valid only for as long as the dualism persists. Analysis of the turning point of the Lewis labor supply curve and subsequent developments is excluded here, as it was by Lewis himself.

III

The discussion has so far proceeded on the assumption that an optimally restrictive trade policy is pursued. It would be useful to briefly examine the consequences of departures from this assumption, with free trade as one alternative and excessive restriction of primary production (in the sense of going beyond the "optimum tariff" point) as the other. In terms of Figure 5.4, the result of following a free trade policy instead of optimum restriction is that the equilibrium point at any instant is at the intersection of the average revenue curve (rather than the marginal revenue curve) with the marginal cost curve. This always results in more primary and less manufacturing production. If specialization continues to be incomplete, the rental on capital will be unchanged from its original position after free trade equilibrium is reached. The capital initially in the primary subsector will earn a higher rental at the margin if the export tax (which can be thought of as the means adopted for the restriction) is lifted, but this will attract more capital until marginal returns are again equated with the manufacturing sector, where the wage rate and marginal product of capital remain unchanged (as a result of the increasing output lowering price) until they fall to the level at which marginal revenue was initially. The capital intensity of production—and hence marginal physical products—are unchanged in both sectors, since these depend solely on the technology and the fixed wage rate. Total capital is fixed at each instant, but a higher proportion is devoted to the primary good under free trade.

At any instant the effect on employment of shifting to free trade depends upon the relative capital intensities of manufacturing and primary production, when specialization is incomplete. Employment increases if the primary product is labor intensive and decreases if it is capital intensive. This result is easily seen in terms of Figure 5.2, since it is the only way in which the changes in output levels determined earlier can be compatible with the fixed real wage rate. In the case of complete specialization, employment always increases under free trade as compared with optimal restriction, since it is the sole means of increasing output with a fixed capital stock. The marginal physical product of labor falls and marginal cost rises. This can be seen from Figure 5.4, since the equilibrium point is shifted from the intersection of the marginal cost curve with the marginal to the average revenue curve, which must be at a higher level.

Total profit at any one time is always reduced as a result of moving to free trade, since marginal revenue is diminishing and equal to marginal cost at the optimal restriction point. With a fixed capital stock this means that the rate of profit—and hence the rate of growth of capital—is also reduced. The familiar conflict between maximizing profit (and with it the potential for increasing output in the future) and employment can thus arise in this model as well, but with the difference—in the incomplete specialization case with manufactures captial intensive—that it comes about through the change in output mix with capital intensities in each branch unchanged instead of as a result of a change in the choice of techniques. Furthermore, if the primary commodity is the more capital intensive of the two the conflict does not arise at all, since the optimal trade restriction results in higher employment as well as higher profits than under free trade.

The question of the convergence of the growth rate of capital to λ or μ discussed earlier is not affected by a whether there is free or optimally restricted trade. The effects of restriction beyond the optimal point are of course simply the opposite in sign of the effects of shifting to free trade and do not require any separate analysis.

The next problem to be investigated is the important one of the consequences of technological change in either branch of the modern sector. The analysis will be confined to discrete or once-over rather than continuous changes in technology and will furthermore be restricted to the so-called Hicks-neutral variety.

Consider first the case of an improvement in the primary commodity when there is incomplete specialization. In terms of Figure 5.4, a Hicks-neutral change in technology would mean that the isoquant tangential to the factor-price line at S has to be scaled up in proportion to the improvement in productivity, so that the length of the vector OS now indicates a higher level of primary production than before, although the resource cost is the same. Since the length of OT indicates the same output of manufactures as before, the marginal cost of a unit of primary output in terms of manufactures has fallen. Relative factor prices remain the same because they depend only on the given real wage rate and the unchanged technology of manufacturing production.

The effect on Figure 5.5 will be to proportionately lower and extend the flat portion of the marginal cost curve, so that the turning point occurs at a lower level and to the right of the original one. Since the marginal product of labor is raised at every level of output, the rising part of the marginal cost curve after the improvement in technology will always be below the original one. The equilibrium output will shift to where the marginal revenue curve intersects the new marginal cost curve and the price falls proportionately to the improvement in productivity, since the fall in marginal revenue is the same as in marginal cost and the demand curve is assumed to have a constant elasticity. Since this constant elasticity has to be greater than unity for the model to be meaningful, it follows that the increase in equilibrium primary output will be proportionately greater than the extent of the technological improvement. In Figure 5.2 a radius vector of given length will represent more primary output in proportion to the productivity increase, so that a more than proportionate increase requires the primary output vector to lengthen. This means that total employment must increase and that some capital has to be diverted from manufacturing output, which declines absolutely. If the primary commodity were capital intensive, however, there would be a reduction of total employment accompanying the rise in primary and the fall in manufacturing output.

The rental per unit of capital does not change as a result of technological progress in the primary branch when there is incomplete specialization, since it is determined by the unchanged conditions in manufacturing. The marginal physical product of capital in primary production rises, but since price and hence marginal revenue falls in the same proportion equality is maintained. The output-capital ratio in primary production is raised in proportion to the rate of technical improvement, and it was shown that the proportion of capital allocated to the primary branch increases. These results, together with equation (5.4), imply that the rate of profit—and hence the rate of growth of capital—are raised at any instant by a once-over technical improvement in primary production, since r is unchanged, p falls, and b rises in the same proportion, and $\widetilde{K}/K$ goes up. However, the limiting rate of growth of capital is still either λ or μ, both of which are independent of technological progress in the primary branch. While higher at any given moment, the growth rate of capital converges in the long run to the same value that it would have reached in the absence of the productivity increase.

When the limit of the growth rate of capital is μ the rate of profit tends to r the rental per unit of capital, since $\widetilde{K}/K$ declines steadily over time with the numerator growing at the rate of λ and the denominator at a rate always exceeding $\mu > \lambda$. When the limiting solution is balanced growth at the rate of λ the rate of profit is ultimately equal to λ/s, which is independent of the level of technological efficiency in either sector. Together with (5.4) this implies that on the balanced growth path

$$\frac{\widetilde{K}}{K} = \frac{(\lambda - sr)}{s} \cdot \frac{\eta}{pb}$$

which means that $\widetilde{K}/K$ tends toward the right-hand side of the above equation. Since r is unchanged and p falls and b rises in the same proportion, it follows that a technological improvement in the primary sector ultimately leaves the proportion of the capital stock allocated to that sector unchanged.

In the case of complete specialization, technical progress in primary production will again result in a fall in price—since the marginal cost curve is shifted to the right—but not to the full extent of the improvement in productivity. The greater the elasticity of the demand curve, the smaller will be the decline in price. There will always be an increase in output and employment, and the rate of profit will always rise with a given capital stock. In equation (5.2) $\partial Q/\partial K$ and Q/K will each rise in proportion to the increase in productivity with employment fixed, but since employment expands they will rise even more. Price and marginal revenue, on the other hand, fall less than in proportion to the technical improvement so that the rate of profit must go up. The same result also can be obtained by noting that the area between the marginal revenue and marginal cost curves, denoting total profit, is increased as a consequence of the technical change even though the capital stock is constant. The higher rate of profit raises the rate of growth of capital at each instant, but the limiting value remains at λ.

Technological progress in the manufacturing branch will now be examined, restricted as in the case of primary production to once-over change of the Hicks-neutral type. The effect on the price of the primary good in terms of manufactures will be considered first. From the Lerner diagram of Figure 5.4, it can be observed that if relative factor prices are held constant and there is technical progress of a certain rate in manufacturing, proportionately more units of manufactures will be equivalent in cost to one unit of the primary good, so that the marginal cost of the latter increases in proportion to the extent of technical progress in manufacturing. The factor-price ratio, however, will be altered by the productivity increase in manufacturing. At the original capital-labor ratio the marginal physical product of labor in manufacturing rises in proportion to the technical improvement, but the real wage rate remains at its exogenously determined level. Hence the capital-labor ratio must be reduced until the marginal product of labor falls to equality with the fixed real wage. The marginal product of capital is raised in the same proportion as the technical improvement at the original capital-labor ratio and further increased as a result of the fall in the capital-labor ratio necessary to equalize the marginal product of labor to the fixed real wage. The wage-rental ratio, therefore, falls more than proportionately to the extent of the technological change.

If manufactures are relatively capital intensive, the effect of the fall in the wage-rental ratio is to lower the value of a unit of the primary commodity in terms of manufactures. There are thus two effects working in opposite directions on the relative cost of the two goods: the direct effect of the technical improvement is to cheapen manufactures, while the indirect effect, through the relative factor price shift, makes them more expensive. It can however be shown that the direct effect must predominate. The reason is that the fall in the wage-rental ratio reduces the capital-labor ratio in primary production as well, so that the marginal physical product of labor falls in that branch. But the marginal revenue product of labor in primary production must continue to be equal to the fixed real wage in terms of manufactures, so that the marginal revenue, and hence the marginal cost of the primary good in terms of manufactures, must rise to compensate for the fall in the marginal physical product of labor. If manufactures are relatively labor-intensive, the shift in the factor-price ratio works in the same direction as the direct effect of the improvement. In either case, therefore, the effect of the technical change in manufactures is to raise the flat portion of the marginal cost curve of primary production in Figure 5.5. The output of the primary good, therefore, contracts and its price rises in momentary equilibrium. Both branches use more labor-intensive techniques and employment will definitely increase if manufacturing is the more labor intensive of the two branches. In the opposite case, each branch becomes more labor intensive; but since the more labor intensive of the two branches contracts its output, there is an effect working in the opposite direction, which makes the net result uncertain.

The rate of profit is raised at any instant with a given capital stock, since capital earns a higher rental in manufacturing and therefore in the primary branch as well. It is true that monopoly profits from primary exports decline, but this is as a result of the superior opportunities in the manufacturing sector obtained by the capital that is transferred there. For the capital remaining in the primary branch there is merely a shift in the category of the surplus earned from monopoly profit to rental income.

This rise in the rate of profit raises the rate of growth of capital at any instant. Whether or not this rise can be permanently sustained depends upon the relation between the new value of μ after the technical progress in manufacturing has occurred and the unchanged value of λ. If $\mu \geq \lambda$ after the change then the increase can be permanently sustained while if $\mu \leq \lambda$ the growth rate must ultimately fall back toward λ in spite of the increase in manufacturing productivity. This result shows that it is possible for the economy to escape from external dependence and "internalize its engine of growth" by a sufficiently large increase in productivity in the manufacturing sector or a rise in the propensity to save out of profits. In other words the classical forces of "productivity and thrift" do not lose their relevance.

IV

The results of this chapter can now be related to the relevant literature. It can readily be seen that the analysis goes beyond the Seers model, since changes in the terms of trade, technical progress, and the propensity to save are all incorporated within the formal structure of our system whereas they are extraneously introduced in his. As compared with both the Seers and the more sophisticated Bardhan model, the analysis given here can focus on structural change, because instead of a single undifferentiated domestic output separate primary and manufacturing branches of production are distinguished. As compared with Bardhan our model has the dual-economy assumption of a fixed wage rate and variable rate of employment expansion whereas Bardhan has the alternative of a fully employed exogenously growing labor force with the wage rate free to be determined. It could be argued that the assumption made here is of more interest in the developmental context within which the problem of sluggish world demand for primary exports is discussed.

As mentioned earlier there has been considerable general discussion about manufactured exports from developing countries, though to the best of our knowledge there has not been any formal model-building along these lines. The sequence traced in this chapter from primary specialization to import substitution to manufactured exports is foreshadowed by Fei and Ranis (1964), for example, in the literary extension of their schema of development to the open economy in the last chapter of their book. Historical examples of primary exports initially propelling expansion but subsequently declining in relative importance to manufactures easily come to mind. Japan and Sweden are perhaps the best known instances, with raw silk in one case and timber and iron ore in the other.

The results of the effects of technical progress on the terms of trade are in conformity with those of the earlier literature based on the standard static trade model such as Findlay and Grubert (1959) and Johnson (1959) but also extend the analysis to dynamics by relating the technical progress in either branch of production to the rate of profit and the rate of capital accumulation. Lewis (1969) has recently discussed this problem in terms of an ingeniously simple application of the elementary Ricardian model. With labor as the only factor of production and fixed input-output coefficients, let the "center" produce food and steel while the "periphery" produces food and coffee. Then, with perfect competition and free trade, the terms of trade between coffee and steel are determined by the amount of food, the common denominator that they can each command. Under these circumstances a technical improvement in coffee production will simply reduce the steel that it can purchase in the same proportion, leaving the primary exporter no better off than before. In the standard general equilibrium analysis neutral technical progress in the exportable sector will turn the terms of trade against the country but will still raise welfare except in the Edgeworth-Bhagwati case of "damnification" or "immiserizing growth."

Neither the conventional trade-theory approach nor the

Ricardian method adopted by Lewis relates the analysis of the effects of technical progress on the terms of trade to the rate of growth of the developing economy. From the results of the previous section, however, we have seen that technical progress in either sector always initially raises the rate of profit and capital accumulation, but it is only when it takes place in manufacturing that this increase may be sustained permanently. There is therefore some ground for the belief, widespread and persistent throughout the Third World, that manufacturing is in some sense more "dynamic" than primary production for export.

CHAPTER 6

Capital Formation, Employment, and the Real Exchange Rate

IN THE models presented in each of the two preceding chapters the maximization of the growth rate required a particular key price ratio to be set to achieve this objective. In chapter 4 this price ratio was the "internal terms of trade" of food to manufactures, with the external terms of trade as given. In chapter 5 it was the external terms of trade themselves between the primary exportable (over which the country has some monopoly power) and the prices of all other goods (taken as fixed on the world market).

In this chapter the price ratio on which attention is concentrated will be that between the prices of tradable goods in general (all of which will be regarded as exogenously determined) and the price of such nontraded or domestic goods as power, transport, and services. This price ratio will be referred to as the "real exchange rate," since on the "small country" assumption with perfectly competitive free trade it is the only relative price that has significance for the allocation of resources. Changes in the nominal exchange rate—the price of foreign currency in terms of home currency—serve only to alter the prices of tradable goods in the same proportion to each other.

The model to be analyzed in this chapter is closely related to the one discussed in chapter 3 and can be considered as an extension of that model (with some modifications) to an open economy. It is perhaps the most general of all the variants of the dual-economy hypothesis that we have discussed, since the capital goods sector in the earlier models was assumed to be either completely self-sufficient domestically or not to exist at all. Here, together with consumption, it will be assumed to have a domestic and a foreign exchange component. The choice of the proportions between these will depend on the appropriate value of the real exchange rate as defined above. Unlike many programming models that have sought to determine the shadow price of foreign exchange, the present approach is in the context of an economy developing over time and is not confined to a solution for a single period only. On the other hand, by contrast with the few dynamic optimization models involving foreign exchange that have appeared, there is a wider scope for choice in the allocation of resources at each instant. Our approach can therefore be thought of as a sort of compromise between microstatics and macrodynamics in the formulation of a planning model.

The analytical methods employed here stem from the famous twelfth chapter of Dorfman, Samuelson, and Solow (1958). In addition to the original source the interested reader may wish to consult the extensive geometric discussion by Vanek (1968) as well as the relevant chapters of the recent textbooks by Lancaster (1968) and Wan (1971). The former gives a lucid and compact mathematical introduction and the latter a difficult but penetrating survey of further developments.

I

This section will describe the basic production structure assumed, which has some slightly novel and unfamiliar features. A twofold classification is adopted between "tradable" and "domestic" goods on the one hand and between "consumption" and "capital" goods on the other. The distinction between tradable and domestic goods is most sharply made on the basis of transport costs being infinite for the latter and zero for the former. In reality, of course, transport costs for any commodity would be positive and finite, but there is perhaps sufficient difference between commodities at either end of the spectrum to make the idealization adopted a useful one. For further convenience it will be assumed that there is just one homogeneous type of domestic good. This good can be produced in alternative ways, as specified by a neoclassical production function with constant returns to scale, the inputs being labor and the services of a stock of malleable physical "capital."

Any number of tradable goods can be distinguished, but it will always be assumed that there is a fixed world price for each of these commodities at which the country can buy and sell on the world market. The technology for producing each of the tradable goods is also taken as representable by neoclassical production functions with constant returns to scale, with labor and "capital" as the inputs. Together with the assumption that the country is "small," this implies that the individual production functions for the tradable commodities can be collapsed into a single "efficient" technology for generating "foreign exchange." This is illustrated in Figure 6.1, where four isoquants are drawn (one for each type of tradable good distinguished) but all for a level of production equivalent in value to a fixed amount of foreign exchange at the given world prices. The solid line shows efficient combinations of labor and capital for producing the specified amount of foreign exchange. As can be seen, commodity D should never be produced, since an equivalent amount of foreign exchange could always be produced with less of both inputs. If the world price of D were to rise, however, it could of course become economical to produce it for some set of relative factor prices. The inner envelope to the isoquants, the solid line of Figure 6.1, therefore defines a "surrogate" production function for "foreign exchange," since the assumption of fixed prices and constant returns to scale means that the efficient combinations of inputs for producing any level of foreign exchange output will simply be multiples (greater or less than unity) of those for the level of output shown in Figure 6.1. If the number of tradable goods is very large, the surrogate curve in Figure 6.1 can be approximated by a smooth curve.

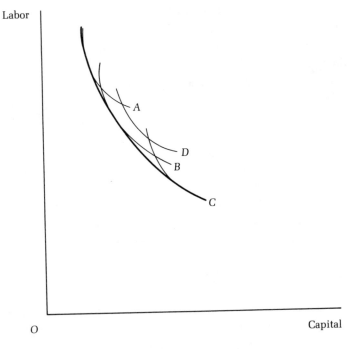

Figure 6.1

Each of the two categories of goods will require some of its own output, as well as of the other, as an input. This problem of intermediate flows can readily be handled by interpreting the capital and labor coefficients in the production functions as "direct plus indirect" requirements, obtained by multiplying the direct inputs alone into the Leontief inverse $(I-A)^{-1}$ of the two-sector economy, so long as it is assumed that there are fixed coefficients relating intermediate inputs to output. The production functions will then be for "net" or "final" output, with all intermediate requirements taken care of.

The consumption and capital goods are regarded as capable of being made by foreign exchange and the domestic good—in alternative combinations as specified by neoclassical production functions with constant returns to scale—with foreign exchange and the domestic good as the inputs of the functions. The foreign exchange and domestic content of consumption and investment are thus regarded as subject to choice and dependent on the relative price of foreign exchange to the domestic good. Production has a two level structure in the model, with labor and capital services producing foreign exchange and the domestic good. These in turn are used to make consumption and capital goods.

Although the consumption and capital goods are directly functions of the domestic good and foreign exchange only, they are indirectly functions of the primary inputs of labor and capital services, by the two level character of the structure of production. The direct production function for each of these goods, specified by an isoquant in foreign-exchange–domestic-good space, can be transformed into an indirect function of labor and capital in the following way. Take any point on the direct isoquant. The combination of foreign exchange and the domestic good at that point will each have a labor-capital isoquant for the corresponding level of production. These isoquants can then be "added" by inverting one of them and sliding it along the other so that a combined isoquant is traced out by the moving origin. Efficiency is maintained by the fact that marginal rates of substitution between labor and capital are equated in the production of foreign exchange and the domestic good. A similar curve can be constructed for each point on the direct isoquant and the inner envelope of all these curves would be the indirect isoquant in labor-capital space corresponding to the given isoquant in foreign-exchange–domestic-good space.

With a given endowment of labor and capital services the production possibilities open to the economy can be readily derived. The alternative combinations of producible consumption and capital goods can be obtained by using either the indirect isoquants in conjunction with the given labor-capital endowment or by first using the latter to generate the production possibilities for tradable and domestic goods and then deriving the consumption-goods–capital-goods possibility set by applying the direct functions. Both methods will, of course, produce the same answer.

If the indirect production functions are used, the method of construction is simply to insert these isoquants into the Edge-worth-Bowley box determined by the factor endowment. By this means the locus that shows the maximum output of consumption goods for each specified level of the capital good may be traced out. In the alternative method the box diagram contains the isoquants for foreign exchange and the domestic good, from which is derived the production possibilities curve MM' of Figure 6.2, showing the maximum level of foreign exchange that can be produced for each specified level of domestic good output.

Each point of MM' in turn determines a box into which the direct isoquants for consumption and capital goods can be inserted and a production possibilities curve for these goods obtained. The outer envelope of all these curves will give the consumption-investment or "absorption" frontier for the economy. This frontier will correspond exactly to the curve obtained by the method employing the "indirect" isoquants. In each case the marginal rate of substitution between capital and labor is equal in the production of foreign exchange and the domestic good and the marginal rate of substitution between these outputs is again equal when they are used as inputs in the production of consumption and capital goods.

In Figure 6.2 the point a on MM' shows the combination at which the output of capital goods takes on the maximum possible value, with no consumption goods produced at all. The point a is where a direct capital goods isoquant is tangential to MM' An analogous point b is obtained where MM' is tangential to a direct consumption goods isoquant, showing maximum possible consumption with zero output of the capital good. Any point between the extremes of maximizing the output of one or the other commodity on the one hand and zero level on the other must lie between a and b on MM' Hence the segment ab is the only efficient region of the frontier MM' Points to the left of a and to the right of b should never be selected. The slopes of MM' at a and b determine the limits on the efficient value of the "real" exchange rate, which is the marginal rate of transformation between foreign exchange and the domestic good. The actual real exchange rate that would prevail is determined once the choice between con-

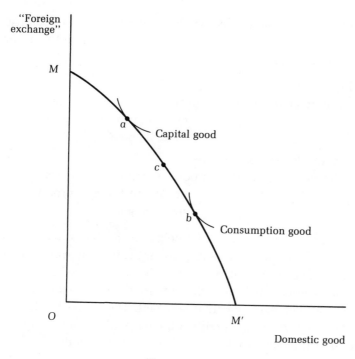

"Foreign exchange"

M

a

Capital good

c

b

Consumption good

O

M'

Domestic good

Figure 6.2

sumption and capital goods is made. This also determines the allocation of labor and capital to tradable and domestic goods, the optimal selection of which tradable goods to produce, and the relative prices of the primary factors, labor and capital services.[1]

Thus suppose that point *c* on MM' is selected as a consequence of the choice made between consumption and investment. The equilibrium real exchange rate will be determined by the slope of MM' at *c*. The coordinates of *c* in Figure 6.2 determine the equilibrium quantities of the domestic good and foreign exchange that

---

[1] With a smooth convex isoquant for foreign exchange only one tradable commodity will be produced, so that there is complete specialization. It should be realized however that this extreme situation will not occur if the isoquant has linear segments and if there are positive transport costs for tradable goods to provide "natural protection" for commodities with domestic unit costs slightly higher than the world price at the optimal factor price ratio.

are supplied and demanded. It should be noted that equality of supply and demand for foreign exchange implies that the balance of trade is zero since

Supply of tradable good
(foreign exchange) = Exports + domestic   absorption
                                    of domestically produced
                                    tradable goods

Demand for tradable goods
(foreign exchange) = Imports + domestic   absorption
                                    of domestically produced
                                    tradable goods

By demand and supply of foreign exchange is meant total demand and supply of tradable goods, valued at world prices, which includes domestic absorption in addition to imports and exports. In other words, it is the potential and not actual conversion into foreign exchange that is meant. The actual levels of exports and imports will depend on the particular commodity composition of the demand and supply of tradable goods.

II

This section presents the simplest possible model of development over time with the "two level" structure of production just described. It will be assumed that labor grows at a constant rate and that a constant proportion of national income is saved and invested. Furthermore, it will be assumed that consumption and capital goods have identical "direct" production functions—i.e., the proportion of foreign exchange and the domestic good used to make a consumption or capital good is identical at every value of the real exchange rate. It will also be convenient to ignore depreciation of capital.

The "direct" production function for the consumption cum capital good in terms of inputs of foreign exchange and the domestic good can be converted, by the method explained in the previous section, into an "indirect" production function in terms of inputs of labor and capital services. The property of constancy of returns to scale will be preserved. The model has now become identical with the well-known neoclassical one-sector growth model of Solow (1956) and Swan (1956), except for the fact that labor and capital do not produce the final consumption-cum-capital good directly but instead produce the domestic and foreign exchange components out of which it is made.

The key relationships of the model can now be readily obtained. The factor endowment and the "indirect" production function for the final good determine the relative factor prices of labor and capital services. The factor endowment itself of course changes over time, in a manner determined by the savings ratio and the growth rate of the labor force. If there is no change in technology or relative world prices for tradable goods, the "indirect" production function would not alter in the course of growth. It follows from neoclassical growth theory that the system will converge to balanced growth at the same rate at which the labor force is increasing, at a capital-labor ratio determined by this growth rate and the savings ratio. By the one-to-one correspondence between the capital-labor ratio and the wage-rental ratio, the latter ratio will rise continually to the level determined by the asymptotic, balanced-growth capital-labor ratio if the initial factor endowment is below this value.

The next important relationship to consider is that between the wage-rental ratio and the relative price of the two commodities produced, which are the domestic good and foreign exchange. This relation has been intensively investigated in trade theory in connection with the factor-price equalization controversy. If foreign exchange is more labor-intensive in production at any wage-rental ratio, then a rising capital-labor ratio implies that the price of a unit of foreign exchange in terms of the domestic good must be monotonically increasing. If foreign exchange is always more capital intensive, then the relative price of foreign exchange will be monotonically decreasing. If the relative factor intensities of the two classes of commodities are such that there are factor-intensity reversals as the wage-rental ratio is varied, then the real exchange rate will fluctuate over time as economic growth proceeds. The price of the labor-intensive commodity always rises (since labor's relative scarcity is always increasing) but which commodity is labor intensive at any moment depends upon the given technology and the factor endowment at that moment.[2] Hence the real exchange rate can both rise and fall in the course of the evolution of the economy to the equilibrium balanced-growth path. The choice of techniques for the production of the domestic good, and the pattern of comparative advantage in the tradable goods sector, however, will always proceed from the labor-intensive to the capital-intensive end of the spectrum since the wage rental ratio is monotonically increasing.

III

The previous section was a digression, intended to illustrate the flexibility of the two level production structure assumed by showing how it can be related to a very familiar type of growth model. For the rest of the discussion, however, we return to the assumption of a dual economy with unlimited supplies of labor at a fixed real wage and with consumption and capital goods differing in the relative intensity with which they require inputs of foreign exchange.

The first section of this chapter described the static solution of the general model, with the levels of the capital and labor inputs fixed and the equilibrium point on the absorption frontier arbitrarily given. This section will link future factor endowments of capital and labor to the present choice of the consumption-investment mix and will determine the necessary intertemporal-efficiency conditions that must hold if development is to proceed optimally.

The stock of capital in period $t + 1$ is simply the given stock in period t plus the output of new capital goods, since depreciation is being neglected. The labor supply in period $(t + 1)$ is equal to

---

[2]This situation can be conveniently depicted by the diagram used by Johnson (1958), chapter 1, figure 1.

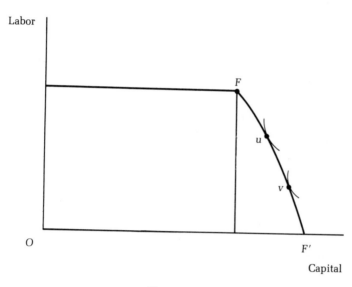

Figure 6.3

the output of consumption goods in period t divided by the fixed real wage rate. The wage bill is thus "advanced" to labor as in classical economics. These relations enable the working of the model to be extended indefinitely into the future. By a simple transformation, the absorption frontier introduced in the first section (showing the consumption-investment choices for period t) becomes a "factor endowment frontier" for period $t + 1$ (showing the alternative capital-labor combinations that can be provided for the next period). The only changes required are that the origin be placed at the level of the existing capital stock, instead of at zero, and that units be chosen such that the real wage rate is one—i.e., a single unit of labor costs a single unit of consumption goods. The vertical axis in Figure 6.3 thus has labor measured on it and the curved part of the factor endowment frontier FF', the portion corresponding to positive investment, coincides with the absorption frontier.

Any one point on FF' will generate a transformation curve between foreign exchange and the domestic good for the next period. The entire frontier FF' therefore generates an envelope

MM' of the individual curves. Each point on *MM'* in turn will generate a transformation curve between consumption and investment; the envelope of all these curves is the absorption frontier
for the next period, which, as explained earlier, can be transformed into the factor endowment frontier. The production process can, therefore, be made to extend indefinitely into the future
for as many periods as desired.

Another way of analyzing the intertemporal production relationships is to use the indirect isoquant maps for capital and consumption goods in conjunction with the factor endowment frontier. The tangency points of *FF'* with the highest attainable
isoquant for each type of final good determines the factor endowment for the next period that would maximize the output of the
corresponding good with zero output of the other. As production
of one good is substituted for the other in the next period, the
desired point on the current factor endowment frontier moves
toward the tangency point of *FF'* with the isoquant map of the
good whose output is rising.

If capital goods are capital intensive and consumption goods
labor intensive, the tangency points would be as depicted in Figure 6.3. A higher capital-labor ratio would be selected on *FF'* if it
is desired to maximize capital goods output in the next period.
Points to the left of *u* on *FF'* would never be chosen and neither
would points to the right of *v*. The efficient segment of *FF'* is
therefore only *uv*. At each of the extreme points *u* and *v* there is
tangency with an isoquant. This implies that the marginal rate of
transformation between capital and labor in the current period is
equal to the marginal rate of substitution between them in the next
period. Since capital and labor used as inputs in one period are
the "outputs" of the system in the preceding period, this condition is the familiar Dorfman-Samuelson-Solow condition that the
marginal rates of transformation between outputs of any two
goods in one period must be equal to the marginal rate of substitution between them when used as inputs in the next.

The intertemporal efficiency condition holds not only at the
end points, but also at all points on the efficient segment of *FF'*.

This can be seen by constructing composite isoquant maps for a fixed level of one output added to all levels of the other by the process of sliding the inverted isoquant for the good with fixed output level along each isoquant in the map for the other and having the corner trace out a "minimum requirements" locus, with the property that marginal rates of substitution are equalized in the production of both goods. Given the level of either good to be produced in the next period, the tangency of the corresponding composite isoquant map with the uv segment of FF' determines the factor endowment that maximizes the output of the other. Thus, here again, there has to be equality between the marginal rates of transformation and substitution.

Let the factor endowment frontiers for successive periods be designated FF' (1), FF' (2), FF' (3), etc. It can be shown, just as in chapter 3, that application of the intertemporal efficiency condition for successive periods results in a continuous narrowing of the efficient segment uv on each frontier. This is because the end points of the initial efficient segment uv on FF' (1) are determined by the end points of the entire curved portion of FF' (2). However, when production is extended to three periods, only a segment of FF' (2) is efficient. This in turn means that only an interior segment of uv on FF' (1) itself is now efficient, and so on. Thus the further away the horizon up to which production is required to be efficient the less open the choice of factor endowment, and hence the consumption-investment mix and real exchange rate, in earlier periods.

This result holds quite independently of the assumption made earlier that the indirect production functions for capital and consumption goods were such that the former was always capital-intensive relative to the latter. For the rest of the chapter, however, this assumption will continue to be made, since the opposite case produces a rather bizarre pattern of development over time. The assumption of capital goods being capital intensive is consistent with either foreign exchange being capital intensive and capital goods foreign-exchange intensive or vice versa. The former case will be assumed to hold in the remaining sections of the chapter.

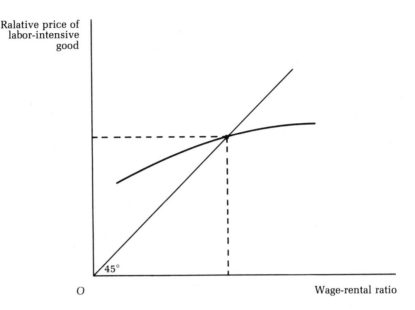

Figure 6.4

IV

The previous section has described the characteristics that an intertemporally efficient path must possess. The focus of this section will be on one intertemporally efficient path that is of special importance—the balanced growth path. After showing that such a path exists and determining the proportions in which production takes place along it, we shall demonstrate that the capital-labor ratio of the economy will converge towards this "Von Neumann Ray" in the long run if production is always required to be intertemporally efficient.[3] The nature of the time path of the real exchange rate and other shadow prices can thus be deduced from this result. These in turn will determine the optimum choices of techniques and comparative advantage at each instant.

The intertemporal efficiency condition requires the marginal rate of transformation between outputs in period t to be equal to the marginal rate of substitution between inputs in period $(t + 1)$.

[3]See Lancaster (1968), chapter 11, section 4 for a proof of the identity of the Von Neumann Ray with the intertemporally efficient balanced growth path.

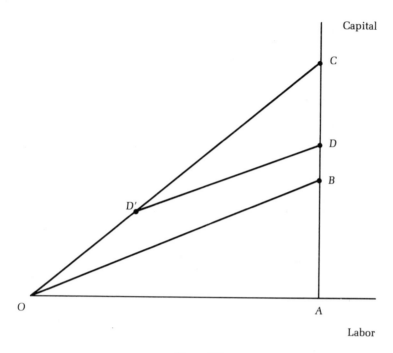

Figure 6.5

Along a balanced path these marginal rates must remain constant. Since relative prices must be equated to these marginal rates, it follows that relative input and output prices must be constant and equal to each other along the balanced growth path. Under the assumptions made here, it follows from well-known results in trade theory that relative output prices will be a monotonically increasing function of relative input prices as shown in Figure 6.4 and that this function will have an elasticity of less than unity.[4] Hence it must be cut by a 45-degree line from the origin so that there is a unique "fixed point" at which relative input and output prices are equal. These are the prices that will hold along the Von Neumann Ray. With relative prices of capital and labor determined, the shadow price of foreign exchange in terms of domestic goods can readily be deduced, by means of a Lerner diagram.

The capital-labor ratio of the Von Neumann Ray is determined in Figure 6.5. The relative prices determined in the manner

[4]See, for example, Kemp (1969) p. 17.

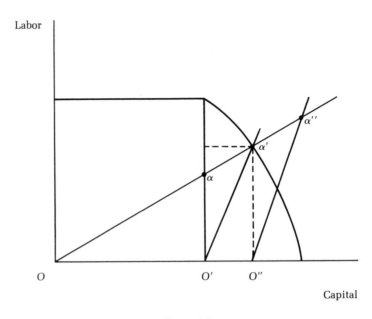

Figure 6.6

explained above will in turn determine the optimal capital-labor ratio to be used in the production of the capital and consumption goods from the indirect isoquant maps for each of these goods. In Figure 6.5 let the length of OA denote one unit of labor and CA and BA the amounts of capital that will be efficiently combined with one unit of labor to produce capital goods and consumption goods respectively, if the Von Neumann price ratio prevails. If the aggregate capital-labor ratio is equal to BA/OA only consumption goods can be produced in an intertemporally efficient way. There can be a positive growth rate of labor if the system is sufficiently productive but there will be zero growth of capital. If the aggregate capital-labor ratio is equal to CA/OA, there will be no labor at all in the next period, but there will be a positive growth rate of capital. Hence in between CA and BA there must be a level of capital per unit of labor at which the growth rates of capital and labor are equal since these growth rates are continuous monotonic functions in opposite directions of the aggregate capital-labor ratio. If this point is D in Figure 6.5, then OD'/DD' measures the proportions in which capital and consumption goods will be produced along the Von Neumann Ray and DA/OA will be the aggregate capital-labor ratio.

With the normalization that one unit of the consumption good buys one unit of labor, the relationship between inputs and outputs can be shown as in Figure 6.6. If α indicates initial input proportions in the optimum ratio, the labor capital ratio will be the slope of $o\alpha\alpha'\ \alpha''$ . . . equal to OA/DA while the proportion of consumption goods (labor) output to capital goods output will be equal to the common slope of $o'\alpha'$, $o''\alpha''$ etc.

The problem now remaining is to show that intertemporally efficient development will tend to the Von Neumann Ray in the long run. This is done with the aid of Figure 6.7, in which the output proportions of capital and labor are plotted as a function of the input proportions of the same variables. Given a capital-labor input ratio it follows from what has been shown earlier that this will determine a family of factor emdowment frontiers differing only in scale. With the "indirect" isoquant maps for capital and consumption goods (labor) it is possible to determine the extreme points of the one-period intertemporally efficient segment on any one of these frontiers. The output proportions corresponding to these points will be invariant with respect to scale. For the point k_1 on the horizontal axis of Figure 6.7, we have the points u_1 and v_1 on the vertical axis, the former corresponding to maximization of capital in the next period and the latter to maximization of labor. As was shown earlier, extending the intertemporal efficiency requirements to successively further periods will move u_1 and v_1 increasingly closer to each other along the vertical line perpendicular to the horizontal axis at k_1.

The relationship between the input and output proportions is further revealed by use of Figure 6.8. If one supposes that the input capital-labor ratio were to be doubled, as shown by a movement from k_1 to k_2 in Figure 6.8, the effect on output proportions will be as follows. In Figure 6.8 an indirect isoquant map, which could represent either output, is drawn together with the factor endowment frontiers corresponding to k_1 and k_2. The vertical distance OL represents one unit of labor. The point of tangency β_1 between F_1F_1 and the relevant isoquant map determines the output

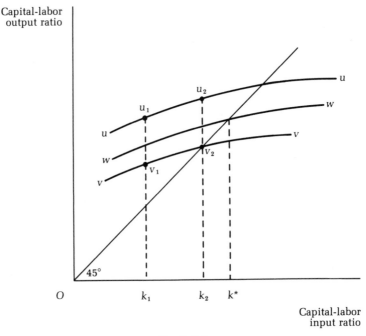

Figure 6.7

proportions u_1 (for capital goods) and v_1 (for labor) shown in Figure 6.7. If the input ratio is doubled from Ok_1 to Ok_2 the factor endowment frontier is F_2F_2. By the Rybczynski theorem the tangent to F_2F_2 parallel to the tangent to F_1F_1 at β_1 will touch F_2F_2 at a point λ such that the output of consumption goods (labor) will be reduced absolutely and the output of capital goods more than doubled. It is clear that maximization of output requires production on F_2F_2 to be to the right of β_2 where F_2F_2 is intersected by the ray $O\beta_1$. Hence raising the input ratio must raise the output ratio of capital and labor. This explains the positive slope of the UU and VV curves in Figure 6.7.

If the elasticity of substitution between capital and labor in producing output is not too high the relative cheapening of capital will not proceed so far as to make the optimal point on F_2F_2 to the right of the point μ where F_2F_2 is intersected by a ray with a slope of half that of $O\beta_1$ corresponding tc a doubling of the capital-labor

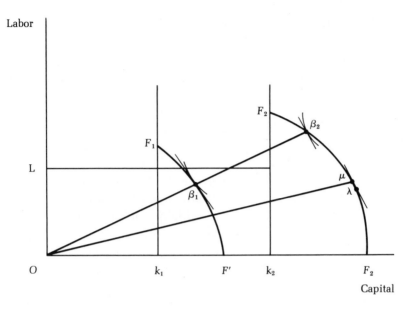

Figure 6.8

ratio.[5] If the tangency of F_2F_2 with the highest attainable isoquant is anywhere inside the arc bounded by β_2 and μ, the output ratio will have risen proportionately less than the input ratio. Under

[5]It would clearly be desirable to have some estimate of how high this critical elasticity of substitution can be. If doubling input proportions exactly doubles output proportions the relevant isoquant in Figure 6.8 will have to be tangential to F_2F_2 at the point μ, so that the slope of F_2F_2 at μ will also indicate the relative factor price ratio that prevails. The proportionate change in the factor-price ratio will therefore be measured by the difference between the slope of the isoquant at β_2 and that of the higher isoquant of the same constant returns to scale family tangential to F_2F_2 at μ. But the slope of the isoquant at β_2 is the same as the slope of F_2F_2 at λ. The proportionate change in the factor-price ratio necessary to induce a doubling of the capital-labor ratio is therefore equal to the proportionate change in the slope of the transformation curve F_2F_2 between λ and μ. This in turn depends upon the extent to which factor intensities differ in the production of the two goods. Johnson (1966) reports that it takes very wide differences to produce small variations in slope. Thus if the order of magnitude of the difference in slope from λ to μ is, say, two percent, the elasticity of substitution required to cause a doubling of the capital-labor ratio will be of the order of fifty. It would therefore seem that the restriction that has to be imposed is not very stringent. It should also be pointed out that the restriction is required by the particular method of proof for convergence that is adopted here and may not be strictly necessary for the result itself.

this restriction the *UU* and *VV* curves of Figure 6.7 must intersect the 45-degree line through the origin only once.

At any input ratio the corersponding points on *UU* and *VV* will move vertically toward each other as the horizon is lengthened and the intertemporal efficiency requirement retained. In the limit the extreme points for each input ratio will converge toward the curve *WW* that lies in between *UU* and *VV*. This curve must have the same properties of positive slope and less than unit elasticity that *UU* and *VV* have. Let k^* denote the value of the input (and output) ratio at which *WW* intersects the 45-degree line. This must be the optimal balanced growth ratio, since it is both balanced and intertemporally efficient. If the initial input ratio is less than k^* the economy will converge asymptotically toward k^* from below in the manner indicated, since the output proportion of one period is the input proportion of the next. If the initial ratio exceeds k^* it will decline toward eventual equality. The system is therefore globally stable.

The more relevant case is obviously the one in which the initial capital-labor ratio is below the Von Neumann value. It is therefore optimal for capital to grow faster than employment and for its shadow price to fall relative to that of labor. This means that the shadow price of foreign exchange must fall over time relative to the price of the domestic good; i.e., the real exchange rate appreciates since foreign exchange is relatively capital-intensive. The pattern of comparative advantage shifts to increasingly capital-intensive tradable goods. All of these movements are bounded by the corresponding values of the variables on the Von Neumann path, which they approach asymptotically from their initial levels. The Von Neumann values therefore serve as upper limits on the possible efficient levels of the capital-labor ratio, real exchange rate, and capital intensity of exportable goods. The direction of movement of these variables seems to be in accord with general expectation, which associates development with capital deepening and which sees the scarcity of foreign exchange as particularly intense in the earlier phases of development, requiring the foreign exchange content of consumption and investment to be kept as low as possible before gradually being eased as development proceeds. Such well-behaved results would not follow if the assumptions about relative capital and foreign exchange intensities were altered. Convergence to the Von Neumann values would still take place but would involve oscillations.

An alternative pattern of development to the asymptotic approach to the Von Neumann Ray is to follow the Ray from the beginning, getting the right proportions by disposing of the labor available in excess of the amount required, given the initial capital stock. Winter (1967) has shown that the longer the horizon the less proportionately is the loss resulting from this simple strategy of "riding the turnpike" in comparison with the true optimal path. Shadow prices, techniques of production, and efficient patterns of specialization would all remain unchanged over time on this strategy. One hitch of course is that disposal of the excess labor force may not be socially "costless," unlike the case with physical or natural resources. Also, if the actual capital-labor ratio in the initial situation diverges sharply from that of the Von Neumann Ray the loss of output involved would be relatively large and would require a long time to recoup.

V

This final section will briefly relate the analysis of this chapter to some of the relevant recent literature. Most studies of development assume either a completely closed economy or a completely open one, in the sense that all goods are tradable on the world market, usually at fixed prices. Bent Hansen (1967) has given a brief but elegant analysis of the completely open economy, but does not push the treatment of nontraded goods and the real exchange rate much beyond noting the limitations of the Tinbergen semi input-output method for this purpose. Corden (1971) uses a two-level production structure with capital and labor producing an exportable and an importable, which in turn combine in different proportions to produce a consumption and an investment good. With fixed world prices this means that capital and labor can be thought of as producing "foreign exchange" as explained in this chapter, which in turn goes to the making of the final consumption and investment goods; but there is no domestic good and hence no real exchange rate. Lefeber (1971) has a dual economy model with consumption and investment goods either exported or imported at fixed world prices. His model, and even a more elaborate one with any number of tradable goods with fixed world prices, can therefore be reduced to the original simple Lewis model with foreign exchange as the sole commodity. With a fixed real wage, perfect competition and free trade will maximize profit (and hence investment and the rate of growth) if all profits are saved and all wages are consumed; but free trade will not maximize output, employment, and consumption if there is a wage differential between the "modern" and the "subsistence" sector. An optimum wage subsidy would therefore raise welfare in the short run at the expense of long-run growth. An optimal shadow wage balancing these alternatives can be worked out, as by Little and Mirrlees (1969). It is somewhat ironic to note that in this situation the traditional comparative advantage approach and the maximum growth approach will coincide.

Little and Mirrlees provide some discussion of how the prices of nontraded goods should be determined for purposes of project appraisal, but they do not focus explicity on the movement of the shadow real exchange rate over time. Chenery, Manne, and others have dealt with the problem of pricing foreign exchange in programming models but these have usually been in the context of a single period. Bacha and Taylor (1971) give a useful survey of alternative approaches to the practical estimation of shadow exchange rates for short-run planning purposes.

Nelson (1970) has presented a model that can be shown to be a simple special case of the approach adopted in the present paper, after some unnecessary obscurities are removed from his interesting discussion, which is inspired by Colombian experience. What makes his model so simple in essentials is that the economy is assumed to produce only a nontraded good, with external aid the sole source of the economy's supply of foreign exchange. The given endowment of capital stock and labor will determine the output of the domestic good from the neoclassical production function that he assumes. Together with the externally given supply of foreign exchange and production functions for consumption and investment goods in terms of inputs of foreign exchange and the domestic good, this will determine a box diagram and hence a production possibilities curve between consumption and investment. Relative factor prices, and their absolute levels in terms of the domestic good, are determined independently of the supply of foreign exchange by the production function and domestic factor endowment. The capital-output ratio in the production of the domestic good will therefore also be determined, and after division by the level of domestic output this enables the axes of the production possibilities curve to be transformed into the rate of growth of domestic output and the ratio of total consumption to domestic output. Choice of a point on this frontier will determine the optimal real exchange rate by the common slope of the tangential isoquants at the corresponding point on the efficiency-locus of the box diagram. Real factor prices in terms of foreign exchange are therefore also determined.

Nelson does not go into the question of the sustainability of the growth rate that has been selected. The critical variable here is the rate of growth of the exogenously supplied foreign exchange. If this is forthcoming at the same rate that the authorities have selected for domestic output, there will be balanced growth at this steady rate with all relative prices unchanged. If it is less, however, it is easy to show that either the growth rate of domestic output must decline to equality with the rate of growth of foreign aid or that real wages must continually decline in terms of foreign exchange, since they are fixed in terms of domestic output and the real exchange rate must depreciate to compensate for the slower growth of available foreign exchange. If the minimum real wage is taken as given, as in the present chapter, the system will be overdetermined and at best one of the three variables—real wage, desired growth rate of domestic output, and growth rate of foreign aid—will have to be adjusted to the other two.

As was mentioned earlier this chapter can be regarded as extending the approach of chapter 3 to an open economy with nontraded goods instead of a completely closed system. We demonstrated in Part One that the Feldman-Domar-Mahalanobis model's stress on investment in the capital goods sector was increasingly desirable the longer the horizon adopted depended upon the crucial assumption of labor not being a scarce factor of production to the modern sector. The essential features of that model were retained in some contributions to development planning in an open economy with a fixed annual flow of foreign exchange available to it. The main references here are Raj and Sen (1961), chapter 8 of Bardhan (1970) and Atkinson (1969)—who gives an especially illuminating formulation. This literature adopts a triangular production structure in which the final consumption good is made by machines that in turn are made by machine tools. It is shown that the priorities in the allocation of foreign exchange and investment shift increasingly to the higher stages of production the further away the horizon at which the value of the terminal capital stock or output is to be maximized. The reason again of course is that there is no feedback from consumption to machine tools, as there is in our own models.

In conclusion we may indicate how the analysis of this chapter, in spite of its abstract character, may perhaps be of some use in interpreting empirical phemomena. In his recent study on the economic development of Argentina, Diaz Alejandro (1970) devotes a great deal of attention to the observed fact that in spite of the rise in saving rates that have taken place in that country since World War II, the rate of real capital formation has not increased significantly, because of the sharp rise in the relative price of capital as compared with consumer goods. For a closed economy this could be explained by relatively low productivity in capital goods industries. For a highly open economy such as Argentina's, however, foreign trade is an important part of the problem. Diaz Alejandro emphasizes this point. His explanation can be reinterpreted in terms of our model if we state it as follows. A combination of exchange rate and domestic policies has placed the economy at such a point on the foreign-exchange–domestic-goods transformation curve that a relative neglect of the former is created. Because of this neglect the absorption frontier generated by this "wrong" output mix has resulted in less investment for given consumption than could have been obtained with the frontier generated by the mix corresponding to the optimal choice of the real exchange rate, capital goods being relatively foreign-exchange intensive. This points to a frequent inconsistency between the Third World's desire for rapid growth through stress on investment on the one hand and the penchant for directly and indirectly subsidizing activities that reduce the potential availability of foreign exchange on the other.

Part Three

COMPARATIVE ADVANTAGE

Factor Proportions,
Capital Rigidity,
and Effective Protection

CHAPTER 7

Factor Proportions and Comparative Advantage in the Long Run

THAT COUNTRIES would specialize in accordance with their "comparative advantage" under free trade, and furthermore that this would generally maximize national welfare, is at the same time perhaps the most beautiful and the most controversial proposition in economic theory. The standard expositions of the theory—from the original formulations by Torrens and Ricardo down to the leading modern writers such as Ohlin, Haberler, Viner, Samuelson and Meade—look at the pattern of international specialization in what may be called a "horizontal" way, with the countries just happening to differ in the relative efficiences with which different commodities could be produced at the margin in isolation. The mutual gain to all parties from specialization and exchange is what is stressed.

This view of the matter, however, has always been challenged by writers who by contrast have adopted a "vertical" perspective, in which manufacturing activities are seen as "higher" on the scale of development than primary production. These writers have frequently come from the less developed parts of the world of their day. Among the writers are Hamilton, List, Manoilesco, and Prebisch, to take only the most obvious examples. In the evocative phrase of Balogh (1963) the participants in the system of international exchange are "unequal partners." The antiseptically neutral process envisioned in the usual blackboard diagram in which "Country A" moves further along the "Commodity X' axis of its transformation curve while "Country B" moves further along the "Commodity Y" axis (both parties gaining by exchange) may look very different when it is realized that X may involve automated factory production and Y backbreaking labor in the cane fields. Radicals see the doctrine of comparative advantage as an ideological cover for the process whereby the vampire of imperialism sucks the blood of the Third World. The recent export of human blood from Haiti makes this something more than a metaphor.

In the Heckscher-Ohlin model the basis of comparative advantage is sought in the differing factor proportions with which the countries are endowed. This at once suggests that comparative advantage can change over time as factor proportions are altered by the accumulation of capital and the growth of the labor force. This has already been demonstrated in the dual economy models of chapters 5 and 6. In chapter 5 the economy could start with complete specialization on a primary exportable and end up with the production of this commodity becoming increasingly negligible relative to manufacturing, which develops from import substitution to take a progressively larger share of growing total exports. In chapter 6 the rising capital-labor ratio and falling real exchange rate or shadow price of foreign exchange shift the optimal pattern of specialization in tradable goods in an increasingly capital-intensive direction, bounded by the values of those variables which prevail on the Von Neumann Ray.

The Heckscher-Ohlin model has been extended by Oniki and Uzawa (1965) to accommodate growth.[1] In this contribution the two goods were identified respectively with consumption and capital goods, and it was shown that convergence to balanced growth in the two-country world economy would take place if the capital good was relatively more labor-intensive. Both countries are of course assumed to have the same exogenously given growth

[1]See also Bardhan (1970), chapter 2.

rate of labor, since otherwise a balanced growth solution could not exist.

In this chapter we shall abandon the dual economy hypothesis in favor of full employment of an exogenously growing labor force as in the Oniki-Uzawa model. We shall simplify greatly by assuming a single small country facing fixed terms of trade instead of dealing with the extremely complex patterns of specialization that result in the general two-country model. On the other hand a third good is introduced into the model in the form of a nontraded capital good, which gives the model some of the features contained in a contribution by Kenen (1965) in which capital augments the productivity of domestic labor and land rather than taking the form of a concrete "thing," such as a machine that can be exported or imported. A paper by Komiya (1967) in which a nontraded good is introduced into the usual static model should also be mentioned.

I

Let us assume an economy that produces three types of goods, denoted by X Y, and Z. Let X and Y be consumer goods and Z a capital good. Each of the three goods is produced by the services of labor, which is exogenously given, and capital, which is the stock of goods of type Z available to the economy. The production function for each good is taken to be of the usual neoclassical type, with constant returns to scale. The growth rate of labor is also exogenously fixed, and for simplicity it is assumed that capital goods do not depreciate. Capital goods are assumed not to move in international trade, but the consumer goods X and Y can be bought and sold in the world market at fixed prices.

The fixed prices of X and Y in world trade indicate that the domestic production costs of amounts of X and Y that have the same value at these prices must be the same, assuming perfect competition and the absence of transport costs and tariffs. If the "strong factor-intensity assumption" that one commodity is always more capital intensive than the other at any factor-price ratio is also made, then it is a well-established result that factor prices will be uniquely determined. The capital-labor ratio in the non-traded capital goods sector will hence be determined, along with those for the two consumer goods sectors. The fixed international terms of trade for X and Y therefore fix the capital and labor input coefficients for all three commodities. Physical units can be chosen in such a way that the prices per unit of each commodity are all equal to unity. Taking the initial endowment of capital and labor as given, we have two equations in three unknowns (X, Y and Z) by the balance conditions that the amount of each factor used in all three sectors must add up to the amount available, the capital and labor input coefficients per unit of each output in these equations being determined by the fixed terms of trade and the production functions. One more equation is needed to close the system, and this is provided by the condition that the proportion of national income saved and invested be a constant. Since investment is nothing but the output of Z, this condition implies that the ratio of the output of Z to the combined output of all three sectors is equal to a constant, which is the average propensity to save.

We therefore have the following system of equations:

$$a_{11}X + a_{12}Y + a_{13}Z = L \tag{7.1}$$

$$a_{21}X + a_{22}Y + a_{23}Z = K \tag{7.2}$$

$$-sX - sY + (1-s)Z = 0 \tag{7.3}$$

in which L and K are the initial endowments of labor and capital, the a_{ij}s are the technical coefficients determined in the manner explained, and s is the average propensity to save. This system is readily solved for X, Y, and Z, given L and K. For the analysis of growth, however, it is necessary to adjust (7.1), (7.2), and (7.3) by dividing both sides of each equation by K to obtain

$$a_{11}\frac{X}{K} + a_{12}\frac{Y}{K} + a_{13}k = \lambda \tag{7.4}$$

$$a_{21}\frac{X}{K} + a_{22}\frac{Y}{K} + a_{23}k = 1 \tag{7.5}$$

$$- s\frac{X}{K} - s\frac{Y}{K} + (1 - s) \, k = 0 \tag{7.6}$$

where $k = Z/K$ and $\lambda = L/K$. Therefore, k is the rate of growth of capital since Z represents additions to the capital stock. The solution of this system can give us k, the rate of growth of capital as a function of λ, the labor-capital ratio.

By Cramer's Rule we have

$$k = \frac{\lambda s(a_{22} - a_{21}) - s \, (a_{12} - a_{11})}{\Delta} \tag{7.7}$$

where

$$\Delta = (1 - s)(a_{11}a_{22} - a_{21}a_{12}) - s(a_{12}a_{23} - a_{22}a_{13}) \\ + s(a_{11}a_{23} - a_{21}a_{13})$$

The problem that now arises is whether k will converge to the constant growth rate of the labor force, n. If $k > n$ then λ will be falling, and convergence requires $dk/d\lambda > 0$. That is, if the growth rate of capital is faster than labor, the system operates to reduce it and vice versa, so that the two rates are equal in the limit. Differentiating (7.7) with respect to λ we obtain

$$\frac{dk}{d\lambda} = \frac{s(a_{22} - a_{21})}{\Delta} \tag{7.8}$$

We shall now investigate the sign of this derivative. A sufficient condition for this derivative to be positive—and hence for the two rates to converge—is easily obtained. If the capital good Z is more capital intensive than X but less capital intensive than Y, it follows that the determinant Δ will be positive. Figure 7.1 shows that under these conditions we must have $a_{22} > a_{21}$. Reversing the relative capital intensities of X and Y will make Δ negative and $a_{22} < a_{21}$, so that the sign of (7.8) is again positive. Hence a sufficient condition for the convergence of the capital growth rate to that of the labor force is for the capital intensity in the nontraded capital goods sector Z to be between those of the traded consumer goods sectors X and Y. If Z is either more or less capital intensive than both X and Y, the sign of (7.8) is indeterminate.

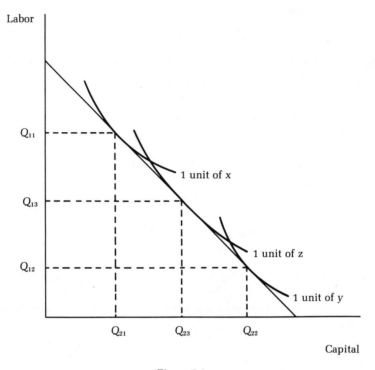

Figure 7.1

II

Now that we have resolved the problem of convergence to long-run equilibrium factor proportions, we shall analyze the pattern of comparative advantage under given demand conditions. The system can also be solved for X/K and Y/K. Division of one by the other will give us the ratio of the outputs of the two consumer goods,

$$\alpha = \frac{X}{Y} = \frac{[(1-s)a_{22} + sa_{23}]\lambda - [(1-s)\,a_{12} + sa_{13}]}{[(1-s)a_{11} + sa_{13}] - [(1-s)\,a_{21} + sa_{23}]\lambda} \qquad (7.9)$$

which gives us the output proportions α as a function of the factor proportions λ.

Demand conditions for X and Y have now to be introduced. As shown by R. Robinson (1956) and Jones (1956–57), the Heckscher-Ohlin theory requires "homothetic" demand patterns for its logical validity—that is, the proportions of the goods purchased at any price ratio must be independent of the level of income. We thus have

$$\beta = \frac{X}{Y} = f\left(\frac{Px}{Py}\right) \tag{7.10}$$

where Px/Py represents the relative prices or terms of trade and β represents the proportion in which the two goods are demanded. Equation (7.9) can be written as $\alpha = g(\lambda, s, Px/Py)$.

Hence, whether a country exports X or Y—that is to say whether it has a comparative advantage in X or Y—depends on whether

$$\alpha \gtreqless \beta \tag{7.11}$$

at the given value of the terms of trade. Since α depends on λ, which varies over time, there is the possibility that the inequality in (7.11) can reverse itself in the course of time. The comparative advantage of a country in international trade is thus not something fixed but something changing with the evolution of its factor proportions.

The analysis of relative stability can now be combined with the definition of comparative advantage given in (7.11) to form the concept of comparative advantage in the long run. If the factor-intensity condition is met, we have seen that the system tends to balanced growth of capital and labor at the fixed rate n. Since $k = n$ in the limit, we can solve (7.7) for the value of λ, to which the system tends in terms of s, n, and the technical coefficients.

Denoting the value of λ in the limit by λ^*, this gives

$$\lambda^* = \frac{\Delta n + s(a_{12} - a_{11})}{s(a_{22} - a_{21})} \tag{7.12}$$

If α^* denotes the value of α corresponding to λ^*, whether the country has a comparative advantage in the long run in X or Y depends on whether

$$\alpha^* \gtreqless \beta \tag{7.13}$$

Since α^*, unlike α, is a constant, comparative advantage in the long run does not shift over time at given terms of trade.

The "dynamic" version of comparative advantage developed above can now be related to the familiar static Heckscher-Ohlin theorem. Equation (7.9) gives us α^* as a function of λ^*. Differentiating, we obtain

$$\frac{\partial \alpha^*}{\partial \lambda^*} = \frac{(1-s)\Delta}{D^2} \tag{7.14}$$

where D is the denominator of the right-hand side of (7.9). The sign of this derivative clearly depends on the sign of Δ. If X is more labor intensive than Y, Δ will be positive, meaning that the more labor-abundant the country, the greater will be the proportion of the labor-intensive good in production at given terms of trade. If demand conditions are homothetic and the same in all countries, this implies that the labor (capital)-abundant country will have a comparative advantage in the labor (capital)-intensive good. The same result would follow if Y is the labor-intensive good and Δ is negative. The familiar Heckscher-Ohlin theorem is thus derived in a more general setting, including the production of a nontraded capital good. The above analysis can be adapted to the usual case simply by putting Z equal to zero.

III

The Heckscher-Ohlin theorem stops at factor proportions as the fundamental determinant of trade. However, we have shown in (7.12) that the factor proportion λ ultimately depends on the "dynamic determinants" s and n. The effect of these variables on comparative advantage can be analyzed by differentiation of (7.12) with respect to each of them:

$$\frac{d\lambda^*}{dn} = \frac{\Delta}{s(a_{22} - a_{21})} \tag{7.15}$$

The sign of this expression is positive, since both numerator and denominator will be positive if X is more labor intensive, or negative if the opposite is the case. From (7.14) we have seen that

α varies directly with λ, so it follows that the greater the rate of growth of labor the greater will be the proportion of the labor-intensive commodity in production in the long run and, therefore, the greater the likelihood that the country will have a comparative advantage in the labor-intensive commodity.

Differentiating (7.12) with respect to s we obtain

$$\frac{d\lambda^*}{ds} = \frac{-(a_{22} - a_{21})(a_{11}a_{22} - a_{21}a_{12})n}{[s(a_{22} - a_{21})]^2} \tag{7.16}$$

From the factor-intensity assumptions the two terms in the numerator of (7.16) are either both positive or both negative, so that in either case the effect of a higher propensity to save is to reduce the labor-capital ratio toward which the system tends in the long run.

The effect of the propensity to save on comparative advantage is given by differentiating (7.9) totally with respect to s to obtain

$$\frac{d\alpha^*}{ds} = \frac{\partial \alpha^*}{\partial s} \bigg| \lambda^* = \text{constant} + \frac{\partial \alpha^*}{\partial \lambda^*} \frac{d\lambda^*}{ds} \tag{7.17}$$

The last two terms have already been obtained in (7.14) and (7.16). The first term is given as

$$\frac{\partial \alpha^*}{\partial s} \bigg| \lambda^* = \text{constant} = \frac{(a_{22} - a_{21})a_{23}\lambda^{*2} + [(a_{11} - a_{12})a_{23}}{D^2}$$

$$- \frac{(a_{22} - a_{21})a_{13}]\lambda^* + (a_{12} - a_{11})a_{13}}{D^2} \tag{7.18}$$

where D is the denominator of the right-hand side of (7.9). What (7.18) shows is the direct effect of the variation in s on α^* through the shift in resources toward the capital goods sector and away from the consumer goods sector. Obviously, if the resources are withdrawn in the same proportion, α^* will not change directly as a result of the variation in s. This will be the case if the labor-capital ratio in the Z sector is exactly equal to that of the whole economy, so that $\lambda^* = a_{13}/a_{23}$. Inserting this value of λ^* into (7.18), we observe that the numerator becomes zero, confirming our intuition. If the labor-capital ratio in the Z sector is higher than λ^*, an increase in the output of Z due to a higher s will reduce the labor-capital ratio in the combined X and Y sector, and hence shift α^* in favor of the relatively capital-intensive consumer good, and vice versa in the case where the labor-capital ratio in Z is lower than λ^*. This can again be checked against (7.18) by differentiating the numerator of this expression with respect to λ^* and evaluating this derivative at the point $\lambda^* = a_{13}/a_{23}$ to obtain

$$\frac{dN}{d\lambda^*} = (a_{22} - a_{21})a_{13} + (a_{11} - a_{12})a_{23} \qquad (7.19)$$

where N is the numerator of the right-hand side of (7.18). Each of the expressions in parentheses will be positive if X is more labor intensive than Y, and negative in the opposite case. Thus, if $\lambda^* < a_{13}/a_{23}$ and X is more labor intensive than Y, the sign of (7.18) will be negative so an increase in s reduces α^* (the output of the capital-intensive good X), and vice versa when $\lambda^* > a_{13}/a_{23}$. If Y is more labor intensive than X, these results will be reversed. If we call the first term of (7.17) the "direct effect" and the second term the "indirect effect," we observe that both terms either move in the same direction to shift α^* in favor of the capital-intensive good or the direct effect works in the opposite direction, so the result depends on which of the two effects is stronger. If the direct effect were to predominate a higher s, and therefore a lower λ^* or labor-capital ratio, would be associated with a higher ratio of the output of the labor-intensive commodity to that of the capital-intensive one; in other words the Leontief Paradox. It would therefore be of some interest to see whether this case can arise, since it would provide another possible explanation of the famous paradox.

If we substitute the right-hand side of (7.12) for λ^* in (7.18) and combine the result with the right-hand sides of (7.14) and (7.16), we obtain:

$$\frac{d\alpha^*}{ds} = \frac{\Delta^2 \, (a_{22} - a_{21})(a_{23}n - 1)n}{[s(a_{22} - a_{21})]^2 D^2} \qquad (7.20)$$

The term $(a_{23}n - 1)$ must be negative, since $1/a_{23} = Z/K_z > n = Z/(K_x + K_y + K_z)$, where the Ks refer to the total capital input in each of the sectors. The last equality holds because the capital growth rate converges to n in the limit. The sign of $(a_{22} - a_{21})$ is positive or negative depending upon whether X or Y is the more labor intensive. Hence the result in either case is that a higher s must be associated with a higher relative output of the capital-intensive good. The Leontief Paradox thus cannot arise as the result of the introduction of a nontraded capital goods sector, but only in the long run. A higher s can cause a lower labor-capital ratio to be associated with a higher relative output of the labor-intensive good as a result of the direct effect, but if sufficient time is allowed the higher s will reduce the labor-capital ratio further until the opposite is the case, if n is the same in both cases.

CHAPTER 8

Capital Rigidity, Import Substitution, and Optimal Intervention

THE PRECEDING chapter has shown how the pattern of comparative advantage can change over time in response to the alteration of factor proportions resulting from capital accumulation and population growth. In contrast with traditional static comparative advantage it put forward a concept of "dynamic" comparative advantage in terms of the factor proportions that would ultimately prevail, given the terms of trade, the propensity to save, and the rate at which the labor force expands. In the model of chapter 6 the pattern of comparative advantage that prevails on the Von Neumann Ray, toward which the economy tends, could also be identified with "dynamic" comparative advantage.

In these models, however (and in the related works of Oniki-Uzawa and Bardhan cited earlier), the dynamic path along which changes in the pattern of comparative advantage take place is simply a succession of static equilibria. The optimum thing to do at each instant is to follow the dictates of the traditional static model. No rationale for deliberate intervention by the state in the process of import substitution can be derived. Competitive resource allocation at each instant is all that is required.

This suggests that a more significant assumption of traditional trade theory might be the malleability of the capital stock rather than its fixed supply. Capital in the standard model is a mythical commodity, Joan Robinson's "leets," which can be instantaneously and costlessly transformed into whatever form and use are required in response to any change in commodity or factor prices. Below, we shall examine the consequences of assuming instead that once it is installed in either sector of the usual two-good model capital cannot be shifted to the other sector at any cost. All the other regular assumptions are retained, so the different results and implications of the analysis are caused by this feature alone.

I

Let the economy be divided into a sector producing tradable goods, that can be bought and sold at fixed prices on the world market and another sector producing nontradable or domestic goods. The factor endowment of the economy is taken as initially given. It is convenient to assume that the economy is guided by a central planning agency that allocates the resources between the tradable and nontradable sectors on the basis of some criterion external to the present considerations, which are concerned solely with the optimal allocation of given resources within the tradable sector.

There are two tradable goods, X and Y, the former capital intensive and the latter labor intensive in the usual sense. Each of these subsectors has a fixed capital stock, which is not shiftable to the other sector. A fixed amount of new investment, however, is available for allocation to either X or Y, but once the allocation is made, no future shifting is possible. The fixed labor supply can be freely allocated between X and Y. The production functions for both goods are of constant returns to scale with variable input proportions. Initially it is convenient to assume that capital lasts forever and that time is divided into discrete periods. Both of these assumptions will be abandoned in the last section of this chapter.

In Figure 8.1 capital is measured vertically and labor horizontally. OA is the initial capital stock in the X sector, and $O'A'$ the

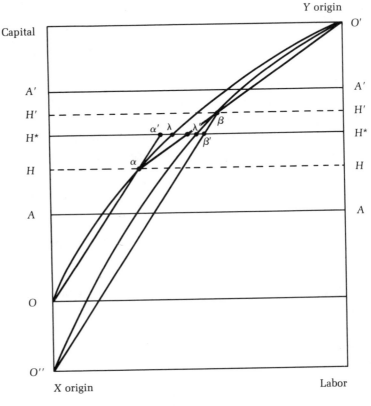

Figure 8.1

initial capital stock in the Y sector. AA' represents the new investment that is capable of being allocated to either sector. OO' would
be the efficiency locus if capital were freely shiftable, but under
the assumptions made here only the segment between AA and
$A'A'$ is attainable. It is assumed that the fixed world prices for X
and Y are such that the value of tradable output at these prices is
maximized at the point α, so that each sector gets some of the
fixed new investment available to be allocated. At α an X and a Y
isoquant are tangential to each other, and the common tangent to
these isoquants determines the shadow factor-price ratio.

Suppose that in the next period there is a further allocation of
new investment to the tradable sector. For simplicity we assume

that the labor force allocated remains the same. If the new investment is equal to OO'', the box diagram for the second period
becomes enlarged, with O'' being the new origin for the X isoquant
map. If the terms of trade were to remain unchanged, and if capital
were fully shiftable, the equilibrium point for the second period
would be β on the efficiency-locus $O''O'$, where the capital-labor
ratios in both X and Y remain unchanged. This is required by the
fact that relative product prices are assumed constant, and hence
relative factor prices and capital-labor ratios must also remain
constant by the one-to-one relationship that holds between product prices and factor prices. It can be seen that the output of the
labor-intensive good Y has contracted, which is the familiar Rybczynski theorem.

Since capital is not shiftable, however, β would not be attainable in the second period if α were chosen in the first period. If investment in Y for the first period were restricted to $A'H'$ instead
of $A'H$, and hence investment in X increased from AH to AH', β
would be attainable in the second period; but this implies that the
value of tradable output cannot be maximized in the first period if
we desire to maximize it in the second.

Fixing the allocation of investment to each sector in the first
period determines the capital stock in each, and a transformation
curve between X and Y is generated as labor is switched from one
sector to the other. There will be one transformation curve corresponding to each particular allocation of investment. Each of
these curves will be entirely within the transformation curve corresponding to OO', which is what would hold if capital were fully
shiftable, except at one point where they would coincide. The
point on each of these curves at which the value of tradable output
in the first period is maximized, subject to the particular investment allocation selected, will be where the slope of the curve is
equal to the given terms of trade.

As investment in Y is increased (and hence investment in X
decreased), the maximum value of tradable output that can be
produced in the first period rises until the allocation corresponding to point α in Figure 8.1 is attained. Beyond that point
the maximum value of tradable output declines up to the point

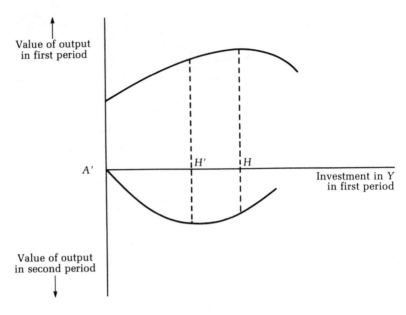

Figure 8.2

where all the investment in the first period is devoted to Y. This relation is depicted in the upper half of Figure 8.2. $A'H$ is the level of investment in Y at which the value of tradable output in the first period reaches the maximum possible level. For this particular allocation of investment ($A'H$ in Y and AH in X) the corresponding transformation curve is tangential to the curve corresponding to full shiftability of capital at the point where the slope of the latter is itself equal to the terms of trade.

Similarly we can trace the effect of the first period's investment in Y on the value of tradable output in the second period. This rises with investment in Y until the point β is attained, after which it declines until all investment is devoted to Y. In Figure 8.2 this relation is shown in the lower half of the diagram. The value of tradable output in the second period reaches a maximum when investment in Y for the first period is at a level of $A'H'$, which is less than AH, the level corresponding to maximization for the first period. The entire investment of the second period is

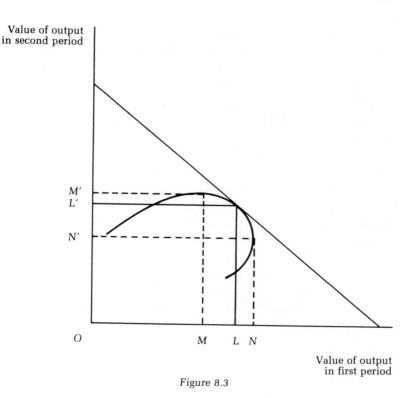

Figure 8.3

of course devoted to X. Figure 8.2 as a whole therefore shows the value of tradable output in both periods as a function of the investment allocation chosen for the first period.

It is clear that the optimum allocation of investment for the first period depends upon the weights attached to the value of tradable output for the two periods. Since the world prices of X and Y are fixed, tradable output in each period can be shadow priced in terms of foreign exchange (say U.S. dollars); it is therefore natural to reduce dollars in different periods to a common denominator by taking the rate of interest at which dollars can be lent or borrowed, assuming that the capital market is perfect and that the country is "small."

Figure 8.3 contains the same information as Figure 8.2, but plotted differently. The axes are the value of tradable output in each of the two periods, and the curve shows how the value of these variables changes as investment in Y in the first period is varied continuously to the maximum possible level. Combination OM and OM' of the value of output in the two periods corresponds to investment in Y of $A'H'$ in Figure 8.2, and the combination ON and ON' to investment of $A'H$. The slope of the straight line tangent to the curve in Figure 8.3 denotes the rate of interest, and the combination OL and OL' gives the values of tradable output for the two periods, which maximizes the present value of all feasible combinations. This maximum occurs at a level of investment in Y that lies between the levels $A'H'$ and $A'H$ in Figure 8.2. It therefore follows that as compared with the optimum two-period solution, maximizing the value of tradable output in the first period alone will result in too much investment in Y and hence too little in X.

If capital were fully shiftable, the combination of ON for the first period and OM' for the second would be feasible, since these values of tradable output correspond to the points α and β in Figure 8.1. This solution would naturally yield a higher present value than the optimal solution for the nonshiftable case. In the shiftable situation the optimum solution would be independent of the rate of interest, since there is no tradeoff involved in maximizing for the first and second periods, because the choice of output mix for the second period is not constrained by the investment allocation for the first period. With nonshiftable capital, the higher the rate of interest, the greater will be the emphasis on raising the value of output in the first period, and hence the greater will be investment in Y in the first period. In other words, the less profitable it will be to deviate from the point α in Figure 8.1.

Let the optimal investment in X and Y be AH^* and $A'H^*$, which correspond to the optimal values of tradable output of OL and OL' in Figure 8.3. It is clear from Figure 8.2 that AH^* must be greater than AH and that $A'H^*$ must be less than $A'H$; i.e., investment must increase in X and fall in Y for the intertemporal optimum to be achieved. The true equilibrium point for the first period in the box diagram of Figure 8.1 must be somewhere along the line H^*H^*. It cannot lie to the left of the point α', where H^*H^* is inter-

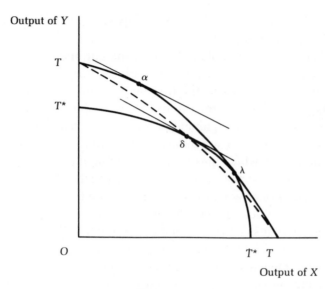

Figure 8.4

sected by the extension of the ray $O\alpha$ from the origin. This is because to the left of α' the marginal product of labor rises in X and falls in Y, whereas at the optimum position labor must obviously have the same marginal product in both alternative uses. Consider now the point λ where H^*H^* is intersected by the efficiency-locus OO' corresponding to the situation with capital fully shiftable. The marginal rate of transformation of Y into X (opportunity cost of the marginal unit of X in terms of Y) is higher at λ than at α. But at the optimal point on H^*H^* the marginal rate of transformation should be the same as at α, since it must be equal to the unchanged terms of trade. Since the marginal rate of transformation of Y into X increases as we move to the right along H^*H^*, the optimal point must lie to the left of λ. Hence it must lie somewhere in the interval between α' and λ.

The same argument can be illustrated by the use of Figure 8.4, in which the transformation curve TT corresponds to the case with full shiftability of capital, and the curve T^*T^* to the situation where the capital stock in X is OH^* and in Y is $O'H^*$. The points α and λ in Figure 8.4 correspond to the same points in Figure 8.1, only they are located in commodity space instead of factor space. The point δ on T^*T^*, where the marginal rate of transformation is equal to the terms of trade, is the optimum point.

It is readily seen that as compared with the fully shiftable case the output of X expands in the first period and the output of Y contracts. This is because the inputs of both capital and labor into X are increased, by the argument of the last two paragraphs, and hence both inputs into Y are reduced. The capital-labor ratio falls in both industries, which means that the marginal product of capital rises in both and the marginal product of labor falls in both. Relative factor prices will not be the same in the two sectors at the optimum point, since we have shown that this point cannot lie on the efficiency locus OO'. An X and a Y isoquant will cross at the optimum point on H^*H^* somewhere in between α' and λ, and the slopes of the tangents to each of these isoquants would indicate relative factor prices in each sector. It is clear that at the optimal point the marginal product of capital will be lower in X than in Y.

The position of the optimum point for the second period can also be located in Figure 8.1. Since all investment in the second period is allocated to X, the optimum point in the second period must also lie on H^*H^*, the investment in X being equal to $O''O$. Consider the point β' where H^*H^* is intersected by the ray $O''\beta$ from the origin. The optimum point cannot lie to the right of β', since this would mean that the marginal product of labor falls in X and rises in Y, and we know that there must be equality at the optimum point. Next consider point λ', where the efficiency-locus $O''O'$, corresponding to full shiftability of capital in the second period, intersects H^*H^*. At λ' the marginal rate of transformation of Y into X (opportunity cost of the marginal unit of X in terms of Y) is lower than at the point β on $O''O'$. At the optimum point, however, the marginal rate of transformation on the transformation curve with $O''H^*$ capital stock in X and $O'H^*$ capital stock in Y must be equal to that of the transformation curve with full shiftability of capital at the point β. It is clear that on the former curve the marginal rate of transformation of Y into X rises as we move to the right along H^*H^*. Hence the optimum point must lie to the right of λ' and therefore in between λ' and β'. This implies that the capital-labor ratio must rise in both sectors as compared with the full shiftability case, and hence that wages must be higher and the return on capital lower than in that situation in the second period. An X and a Y isoquant will cross at the optimum point on H^*H^* between λ' and β', and since this point is to the right of the efficiency-locus $O''O'$, the slope of the tangent to the X isoquant will be flatter than that of the tangent to the Y isoquant. This means that the marginal product of capital in X is higher than in Y in the second period. Since both inputs have increased, the output of Y in the second period must be larger than it would be in the full shiftability case, and the output of X must therefore be smaller. As compared with the first period's output levels, however, the output of X rises and the output of Y falls in the nonshiftable case as well. The reason is that at any point between λ' and β' the output of Y must be smaller than at any point between α' and λ, as a result of the same input of capital and less input of labor being used, whereas the output of X must be higher as a consequence of more of both inputs being used.

II

It may now be useful to give a concise mathematical statement of the rather involved geometrical arguments that have been used so far. It will be realized, however, that the interpretation of the mathematical analysis is greatly facilitated by our having previously gone through the more extended, but intuitively clearer, geometric discussion. The problem can be posed quite simply in the usual constrained maximum form, and the solution obtained by use of Lagrangean multipliers, with the appropriate Kuhn-Tucker modifications when needed. We denote labor by L, capital by K, investment by I, prices by p, and the rate of interest by i. Subscripts denote commodities X and Y and periods 1 and 2.

The objective function to be maximized is the present value of tradable output at the fixed world prices in the two periods, subject to the constraints on the labor force, capital, and investment. The assumption of nonshiftability of capital implies that investment in either sector must be nonnegative, which is, of course, the

constraint that provides the entire raison d'être for the analysis of
this chapter.

The Lagrangean expression is

$$\frac{1}{(1+i)} P_X X_2 [L_{x2}, K_{X2}(I_{X2}, I_{X1})] + \frac{1}{(1+i)} P_Y Y_2 [L_{Y2}, K_{Y2}(I_{Y2}, I_{Y1})]$$

$$+ p_X X_1 [L_{X1}, K_{X1}(I_{XI})] + p_Y Y_1 [L_{Y1} K_{Y1}(I_{Y1})] - \lambda_1 [L_{X1} + L_{Y1} - L_1]$$

$$- \lambda_2 [L_{X2} + L_{Y2} - L_2] - \mu_1 [I_{X1} + I_{Y1} - \overline{I}_1] - \mu_2 [I_{X2} + I_{Y2} - \overline{I}_2]$$

The necessary conditions for maximization are

$$\frac{1}{(1+i)} P_X \frac{\partial X_2}{\partial L_{X2}} - \lambda_2 = 0 \tag{8.1}$$

$$\frac{1}{(1+i)} P_Y \frac{\partial Y_2}{\partial L_{Y2}} - \lambda_2 = 0 \tag{8.2}$$

$$\frac{1}{(1+i)} P_X \frac{\partial X_2}{\partial K_{X2}} \frac{\partial K_{X2}}{\partial I_{X2}} - \mu_2 = 0 \tag{8.3}$$

$$\frac{1}{(1+i)} P_Y \frac{\partial Y_2}{\partial K_{Y2}} \frac{\partial K_{Y2}}{\partial I_{Y2}} - \mu_2 < 0 \quad \text{since} \quad I_{Y2} = 0 \tag{8.4}$$

$$\frac{1}{(1+i)} P_X \frac{\partial X_2}{\partial K_{X2}} \frac{\partial K_{X2}}{\partial I_{X1}} + P_X \frac{\partial X_1}{\partial K_{X1}} \frac{\partial K_{X1}}{\partial I_{X1}} - \mu_1 = 0 \tag{8.5}$$

$$\frac{1}{(1+i)} P_Y \frac{\partial Y_2}{\partial K_{Y2}} \frac{\partial K_{Y2}}{\partial I_{Y1}} + P_Y \frac{\partial Y_1}{\partial K_{Y1}} \frac{\partial K_{Y1}}{\partial I_{Y1}} - \mu_1 = 0 \tag{8.6}$$

$$P_X \frac{\partial X_1}{\partial L_{X1}} - \lambda_1 = 0 \tag{8.7}$$

$$P_Y \frac{\partial Y_1}{\partial L_{Y1}} - \lambda_1 = 0 \tag{8.8}$$

Equations (8.1) and (8.2) state that the marginal value product of
labor must be equalized in both sectors in the second period, and
equations (8.7) and (8.8) state the same thing for the first period. In
interpreting equations (8.3) through (8.6), we first note that all
partial derivatives of capital stocks with respect to investment are
unity, since the increase of investment by one unit increases the
capital stock by one unit. Equation (8.3) therefore determines μ_2,

the shadow rental of capital in the second period, which is equal to the discounted marginal value product of capital in the X sector. Equation (8.4) states that the marginal value product of capital in the Y sector must be less than μ_2, since it is not profitable to invest in the Y sector at all in the second period. Equations (8.5) and (8.6) give μ_1, the shadow price of investment in the first period, as the present value of the rentals of capital in the two periods in either sector. Investment in X and Y in the first period must therefore be carried on in each sector up to the point where the current return plus the discounted future return is equal to the shadow price μ_1.

We know from (8.3) and (8.4) that the first term in (8.5) exceeds the first term in (8.6). Hence the second term in (8.6) must exceed the second term in (8.5) by the same amount since the sum of terms in both (8.5) and (8.6) is equal to μ_1. Hence we find that the optimal solution requires the marginal value product of capital in Y to exceed the marginal value product of capital in X in the first period by an amount equal to the discounted value of the excess of the marginal value product of capital in Y in the second period. This relation can be written as

$$-\frac{1}{(1+i)}\left[P_y\frac{\partial Y_2}{\partial I_{y1}} - P_x\frac{\partial X_2}{\partial I_{x1}}\right] = \left[P_y\frac{\partial Y_1}{\partial I_{y1}} - P_x\frac{\partial X_1}{\partial I_{x1}}\right]$$

The expression on the right-hand side indicates the current net gain from shifting a unit of investment from the X to the Y sector in the first period. The expression on the left is the discounted net loss in the second period resulting from the same action. Optimal allocation requires these two magnitudes to be equal. It is easily seen that the relation above is equivalent to the tangency condition of Figure 8.3.

The labor and investment allocations to each sector for each period give us eight unknowns. When these are added to the Lagrange multipliers, a total of twelve unknowns results. There are four constraints and seven equations from the necessary conditions for maximization. Corresponding to the inequality in (8.4) we have the condition that I_Y is zero. The remaining eleven unknowns are therefore determined by the eleven equations.

III

We now turn to the question of whether the optimal solution can be attained under laissez faire or whether some form of intervention is necessary. We shall attempt to discover whether the planners need to do more than simply determine the total investment levels for each period and leave the rest to the free market or a Lange-Lerner simulation of such a market.

If it is assumed that the decisionmakers at the firm level, whether private entrepreneurs or socialist managers, have "perfect foresight," then no intervention by the central planning body will be necessary. Equations (8.5) and (8.6) will be satisfied, since investors in the X sector will realize that although their current return is less than in the Y sector, they will be compensated by a higher return in the next period. Similarly, investors in the Y sector anticipate that they will earn less in the future than they could if they invested in the X sector, but the current excess return that they receive is sufficient to compensate them for this.

However it is clearly quite absurd to expect that microdecisionmakers can ever be in a position to anticipate perfectly what the situation will be in the next period, since this depends on a change in factor proportions—a change decided upon by the central planners. The "perfect foresight" assumption only makes sense in the setting of a stationary state or a "golden age," in which relative factor prices are either constant or changing at a constant rate. The situation we are dealing with, however, is that of a once-over change, which could drastically alter relative factor proportions. Therefore no basis exists for assuming that the optimal adjustment can be made spontaneously at the micro level.

A more realistic assumption is that firms will act to equalize returns on investment in the current period, as there is no way for the firms to know which sector will prove more profitable in the future. This "myopic" behavior is consistent with optimality over time in the usual model, which assumes full shiftability of capital. As Joan Robinson says, when capital is made of "leets," "there is no difference between the past and the future, for the past can always be undone and readjusted to a change in the present situation."[1] The whole problem of whether or not the expectations are correct therefore disappears.

The free play of the market will therefore produce the optimal solution for the full shiftability case in the first period—i.e., the point α in Figures 8.1 and 8.4—even though capital is not shiftable. As we have seen, this cannot be the true optimum solution under the conditions assumed. Achievement of the true optimum position therefore requires some form of intervention in the form of subsidies or taxes on inputs and outputs. The nature of the optimal intervention required can be readily deduced. In the first period we wish to encourage investment in X beyond the point of equal returns with investment in Y, since as a result of the planned increase in the relative endowment of capital, the X sector will expand in the future and the Y sector will contract. This can be achieved by placing a subsidy on the use of capital in the X sector in the first period. This discriminatory subsidy on capital use in the X sector will mean that investment in X will expand up to the point where the marginal product of capital in the X sector falls short of the marginal product in the Y sector by the amount of the subsidy. As we have seen in the previous section, the difference in marginal productivities of capital between X and Y in the first period must equal the discounted value of the opposite difference between these magnitudes in the second period, which determines the amount of the subsidy. No subsidies or taxes need be placed on either commodity since the marginal rate of transformation on T^*T^* in Figure 8.4 at the optimum point δ is equal to the terms of trade. Because labor is the only variable factor along T^*T^*, the marginal rate of transformation along it is equal to the ratio of the marginal productivities of labor and from (8.7) and (8.8) we can see that this ratio is equal to the ratio of the two fixed world prices of X and Y at the optimum point.

From another point of view it is possible to regard the effects of the subsidy on capital in X as analogous to the effect of a "distortion" in domestic factor markets as analyzed by Hagen (1958), Bhagwati and Ramaswami (1963), and others. This literature

---

[1]Robinson (1970) p. 312.

notes that such a distortion shrinks the regular transformation curve inward and also has the effect of making the marginal rate of transformation deviate from the fixed commodity price ratio at the competitive equilibrium point. The sector that has to pay the lower price for the same factor will expand beyond the point where the marginal rate of transformation is equal to the price ratio of the two commodities.

In Figure 8.4, however, the transformation curve corresponding to the effect of a distortion in the market for capital in favor of the X sector would not be T^*T^* but the dashed line passing through the point δ and coinciding with TT at both end points. The slope of this dashed curve at δ is obviously not equal to the fixed terms of trade, because the output of X has expanded beyond the point at which equality obtains as a result of the lower price of capital at the margin in that sector. Our results for both the optimal point itself and the optimal intervention for achieving it are thus consistent with looking at the problem from the point of view of distortions.

Bhagwati and Srinivasan (1969) examine the problem of how best to secure an arbitrarily set intersectoral allocation of one factor and show that the optimal intervention is a factor subsidy. Our result is thus similar to theirs; the difference, however, is that the required factor allocation is not an independent noneconomic objective but a consequence of maximization over a two-period horizon in a model with nonshiftable capital.

It will be useful to compare this optimal form of intervention with other more obvious ones. A tariff on X is dominated by an output subsidy on X, since the same effect on production can always be secured without cost in terms of restriction of consumption. We shall therefore compare the optimal intervention to an output subsidy on X. The inferiority of an output subsidy on X can be proved with the use of Figure 8.4. With an output subsidy on X only, the marginal rates of substitution between labor and capital will be equal in both sectors, and so production will take place on the transformation curve TT. The marginal rate of transformation of Y into X at the production point will be greater than the relative world price of X, since the price of X to domestic producers is raised by the output subsidy. Let the point λ in Figure 8.4 be the point corresponding to a situation with an output subsidy on X. All points on the transformation curve T*T* have the same investment allocation as at λ, which lies on both transformation curves. The point δ, attainable with the optimal intervention of a capital subsidy in X, is clearly superior to λ, since the investment allocation is the same. This means that the points are equivalent as far as the second period is concerned, while the value of current output at world prices is greater at δ than at λ.

As we vary the output subsidy on X continuously from zero, the value at world prices of current tradable output will fall, but investment in X—and hence the value of the second period's output—will rise. Given the rate of interest, an optimal point can be selected as in Figure 8.3, but this will be a "second best" optimum. A tariff on X can only be a "third best" optimum but could still in principle be superior to no intervention at all.

IV

We shall show in this section how the conclusions derived remain valid when time is treated as continuous instead of discrete and when a positive rate of capital depreciation is allowed for. It will be convenient to use the formalism of the Pontryagin "maximum principle," which has a straightforward economic interpretation in the present case. The following notation will be used:

T = fixed horizon
r = constant discount rate
Px, Py = fixed world prices of X and Y
Kx, Ky = specific capital stocks in X and Y
Lx, Ly = labor allocated to X and Y
Lo = fixed total labor force
μ = constant rate of depreciation of capital stocks
Io = initial gross investment
g = constant rate of growth of gross investment
u = fraction of total gross investment allocated to X
$\lambda x, \lambda y$ = shadow prices of investment in sectors X and Y

The objective function is taken to be the maximization of the integral of the value of output at world prices over a given finite horizon, discounted to the present at a constant positive rate. Gross investment is exogenously given and growing at a constant rate.

Symbolically the problem can be formulated as:

Maximize $\int_o^T e^{-rt} [P_x X(Kx, Lx) + Py Y(Ky, Ly)] \, dt$

subject to

$$\dot{Kx} = uIoe^{gt} - \mu Kx$$

$$\dot{Ky} = (1 - u)Ioe^{gt} - \mu Ky$$

$$Lx(t) + Ly(t) = Lo$$

The "current value" Hamiltonian is

$$H = PxX(Kx, Lx) + PyY(Ky, Ly) + \lambda x[uIoe^{gt} - \mu Kx] + \lambda y \\ [(1 - u) Ioe^{gt} - \mu Ky]$$

where λx and λy are the so-called auxiliary variables interpreted as the shadow prices of investment in the two sectors. By putting $v = Lx/Lo$ and hence $(1 - v) = Ly/Lo$ the control variables can be written as u and v, the proportions in which investment and labor input respectively are allocated between the sectors. The state variables are the capital stocks $Kx(t)$ and $Ky(t)$.

The necessary conditions for the optimal solution to the problem require the Hamiltonian to be maximized at each instant with respect to the control variables, while the state and auxiliary variables are treated as if they were constants. The values of the control variables u and v are restricted to the closed interval between zero and unity. At an interior solution the derivative of the Hamiltonian with respect to the control variable must be zero, whereas it would be negative or zero if the optimal value of the control were zero and positive or zero if it were unity.

These derivatives are

$$\frac{\partial H}{\partial v} = Px \frac{\partial X}{\partial Lx} - Py \frac{\partial Y}{\partial Ly}$$

$$\frac{\partial H}{\partial u} = \lambda x - \lambda y$$

Assuming an interior solution for allocation of the labor force the marginal value product of labor has to be equalized between the sectors at each instant. The rule for allocation of investment is

$$u = 1 \text{ if } \lambda x > \lambda y$$

$$u = o \text{ if } \lambda x < \lambda y$$

$$o < u < 1 \text{ if } \lambda x = \lambda y$$

which simply says that investment should go into the sector where its shadow price is higher until the amount available is exhausted or shadow prices are equalized. The further necessary conditions for an optimal solution require the shadow prices to be changing over time according to the equations

$$\dot{\lambda}x = - Px \frac{\partial X}{\partial Kx} + (\mu + r) \lambda x$$

$$\dot{\lambda}y = - Py \frac{\partial Y}{\partial Ky} + (\mu + r) \lambda y$$

which state that the value of a unit of investment in each sector declines over time at a rate equal to the gross current rental less depreciation and interest charges.

Finally there are the transversality conditions

$$\lambda x(T) = \lambda y(T) = 0$$

which state that the terminal value of investment in either sector at the horizon is zero.

The shadow price differential equations can be solved for $\lambda x(t)$ and $\lambda y(t)$ to yield

$$\lambda x(t) = \int_t^T Px \frac{\partial X}{\partial Kx} (\tau) e^{-(r + \mu)(\tau - t)} d\tau$$

$$\lambda y(t) = \int_t^T Py \frac{\partial Y}{\partial Ky} (\tau) e^{-(r + \mu)(\tau - t)} d\tau$$

showing that the shadow price of investment in each sector at time t is equal to the total stream of rentals from that time up to the horizon T, discounted by the sum of the rate of interest and the rate of depreciation.

Suppose that before the analysis begins the structure of the capital stock is appropriate to the ruling relative prices on the world market so that both labor and capital have the same marginal value product in each sector. Let there now be a sharp alteration in relative world prices in favor of Y, the labor-intensive commodity. In terms of the standard model there is a shift of both factors into Y until marginal value products are again equated, the movement taking place along the efficiency-locus of the box diagram. With nonshiftable capital, however, it is impossible to transfer capital from X to Y in response to the shift in the product-price ratio. Labor, though, can be shifted from X to Y until the marginal physical product of labor in X has fallen, and in Y has risen, sufficiently to offset the shift in the product price ratio in favor of Y, so that the marginal value product of labor is equated in the two sectors. The additional labor on the fixed capital stock in Y raises the marginal physical product of capital in that sector while the opposite is the case in the X sector. Since the relative price of Y has risen, the marginal value product of capital is higher in Y than in X after labor has been reallocated in response to the shift in relative product prices. It should be clear that whenever the capital stock in one sector is less than what it should be in the full shiftability case the marginal value product of capital in the "deficient" sector will be lower than in the other. The signal given by the competitive price mechanism cannot be followed by the existing capital stock because of the assumption of specificity.

However, the deficiency in the optimal sectoral capital stock can be made up by allocation from new flows of gross investment. Insight into the optimal allocation of investment can be provided by comparing the sectoral capital stock at any moment with what it should be if the total stock were fully shiftable, since as we have seen this provides an indication of where the marginal value product of capital is higher. The optimal sectoral capital stock for a given total capital stock, on the assumption of full shiftability, can readily be calculated. The capital and labor coefficients per unit of output in each sector will be constants, since relative product prices are unchanged and there is a one-to-one correspondence between the product-price ratio and the factor-price ratio, with constant returns to scale in both sectors. From the two equations stating that the sum of each factor used in the two sectors must add up to the total available, the corresponding output levels can be solved for, given the technical coefficients. Since output can be expressed as the sectoral capital stock divided by the sectoral capital-output ratio, we can write for the optimal sectoral capital stock in Y, on the assumption of full shiftability

$$\hat{K}_y(t) = \frac{A_{ky}\left[A_{lx}\,K(t) - A_{kx}\,Lo\right]}{(A_{ky}\,A_{lx} - A_{ly}\,A_{kx})}$$

where the A_{ij}s are the labor-output and capital-output ratios. It can be seen that $\hat{K}y(t)$ is a decreasing function of $K(t)$, since the fact that Y is the labor-intensive good makes the denominator negative. $K(t)$ itself, on the assumption of full shiftability, can be obtained by summing the equations for $\dot{K}x(t)$ and $\dot{K}y(t)$ and integrating, to obtain

$$K(t) = \frac{Io}{(g + \mu)}\,e^{gt} + \left[Ko - \frac{Io}{(g + \mu)}\right]e^{-\mu t}$$

where $Ko = \overline{K}x + \overline{K}y$ is the initial total capital stock, which is the sum of the initial capital stocks in the two sectors. With g assumed sufficiently large in relation to μ, $K(t)$ is an increasing function of time so that $\hat{K}y(t)$ is a decreasing function of time, as shown by the downward sloping curve in Figure 8.5, with its intercept at $\hat{K}y(o)$, the optimal capital stock in the Y sector at the moment when relative prices have shifted to the new level at which they remain for the rest of the time.

The actual capital stock in the Y sector, however, is below this value, and instantaneous adjustment therefore cannot be made because of the nonshiftability assumption. The capital stock in the Y sector can however be built up by new investment, and the upward sloping curve starting from $\overline{K}y$ shows the evolution of $Ky(t)$ on the assumption that gross investment is completely allocated to the Y sector, which is to say that a policy of $u = 0$ is followed. The two curves cross at t', the point at which the marginal value product of capital in the two sectors would be equated. From time 0 to t' the marginal value product of capital is higher in Y than in X. It is of course assumed that the horizon is sufficiently long so that $t' < T$.

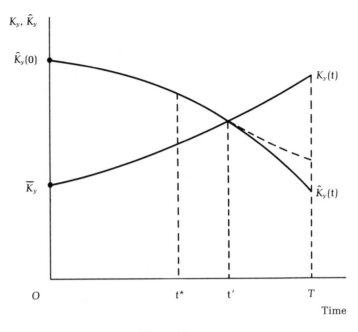

Figure 8.5

The dashed line in Figure 8.5 shows what happens to $Ky(t)$ for $t > t'$ on the assumption that no further investment is made in the Y sector—i.e., $u = 1$. It therefore shows the capital stock in Y running down from its level at t' at the maximum possible rate with zero replacement. It is assumed that g is sufficiently large relative to μ so that the dashed line lies everywhere above the $\hat{K}y(t)$ curve for $t > t'$. In other words we are assuming that the Rybczynski effect of the growing total capital stock in reducing the optimal sectoral capital stock in Y exceeds the rate of depreciation. In this case it is clear that the Y capital stock is excessive after t' if a policy of $u = 0$ is followed from the beginning to t' so that the marginal value product of capital must be higher in X than in Y after t' is passed, which means that $u = 1$ from t' to T.

Let us now consider what would be the appropriate policy at time $(t' - \theta)$ where θ is initially very small. If we make $u = 0$ then for θ time we would get higher returns, since the marginal value

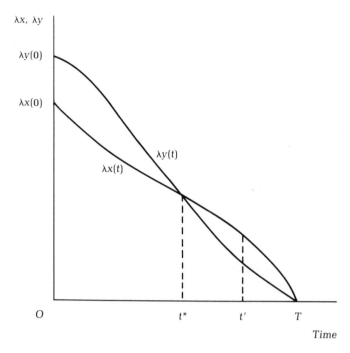

Figure 8.6

product of capital is higher in Y, but for the period $(T - t')$ we would get lower returns, since the relation between the marginal value products of capital in the two sectors is reversed after t'. If θ is sufficiently small the $u = 1$ policy would clearly be superior, since it is only for a fleeting initial segment of time that higher returns are obtained in Y. Afterward, higher returns are obtained in X. As θ is made longer the costs of the $u = 1$ policy will increase up to a point at which it breaks even with the $u = 0$ policy. Thus there is a time t^* before t' at which it becomes optimal to switch from a $u = 0$ to a $u = 1$ policy.

At time t^* the present value of all future returns up to the horizon from investment in each of the two sectors is the same, with the Y sector having a higher current marginal value product of capital from t^* to t' and the X sector from t' to T. The relation between λx and λy must therefore be as depicted in Figure 8.6 with λy exceeding λx up to t^* and the reverse thereafter. What Arrow (1968) has called the "myopic decision rule" of allocating investment on the basis of the current marginal value product alone would therefore not be valid in the interval from t^* to t', where it is optimal to put investment in X even though the current rental would be higher in Y.

The restriction to a discrete two-period model and the absence of depreciation assumed in the first three sections of this chapter have therefore been removed without changing the essential point of the analysis. This essential point may be stated as follows: There is a general presumption among economists that perfect competition will secure an "efficient" solution in the absence of externalities and distortions in the markets for goods and factors. We have shown that this is not necessarily so in a very simple model with nonshiftable capital, unless perfect competition is defined in such a way as to imply perfect foresight on the part of decisionmakers at the microlevel.

The point can also be put with reference to Figure 8.4. The "comparative advantage" solution of conventional trade theory would be the point α, whereas the optimal development policy would be to choose the point δ. Taking Y as the exportable and X as the importable, we have given a rigorous case for import substitution. With an appropriately chosen demand pattern it is also possible that X is exported when the production point is at δ, whereas it is imported when the production point is at α. Alternatively, we could say that α is the point of "static" comparative advantage, while δ corresponds to "dynamic" comparative advantage. In any case, what we have shown is that the optimal current trade pattern cannot be chosen without reference to *future* factor proportions.

This chapter has assumed that the labor force in the tradable sector is held constant. If both capital and labor grow, the contraction in the output of Y need not take place and the tradeoff between present and future analyzed in this chapter would not exist. The standard solution of equating the marginal value product of capital in the two sectors at each point of time could be followed. However, if the rate of growth of capital is sufficiently greater than that of the labor force, the contraction of Y output would still be required, and so the whole analysis would stand. What is required for the relevance of the present analysis is therefore a substantial change in the factor proportions of the tradable sector. Such a situation could clearly exist during a "big push" development program.

CHAPTER 9

Comparative Advantage, Effective Protection, and the Domestic Resource Cost of Foreign Exchange

RECENTLY considerable analytical effort has gone into evaluating the cost of protection. The concept of "effective protection" has played a key role in these developments. Calculations have shown how the escalated tariff structures of the advanced countries have discriminated against labor-intensive manufactures in which developing countries can be expected to have a current or potential comparative advantage. Application of the same concept to developing countries—for example the study by Lewis and Guisinger (1968) on Pakistan—has shown the extreme inefficiency of several manufacturing industries in these countries.

A related concept, which has been employed in similar contexts, is the "domestic resource cost per unit of foreign exchange." This concept attempts to compute the cost of domestic resources per unit of foreign exchange earned in export sectors or saved in import-substituting ones. The concept was originally developed by Michael Bruno (1963) in connection with his input-output and linear programming studies of the economy of Israel and was also used by Anne Krueger (1966) in an evaluation of the cost of exchange control in Turkey. A later contribution by Bruno

(1967) shows how the concept can be used as an investment criterion for the optimal selection of new projects producing tradable
goods. Krueger also looks upon her ex post results for various
Turkish industries as providing a criterion for the allocation of future resources, or reallocation of existing resources wherever
feasible, toward certain export industries where she found the
domestic resource cost of foreign exchange low, and away from
import substituting sectors where it was three to four times as
high. Balassa and Schydlowsky (1968) asserted that the Bruno-
Krueger approach is erroneous as a guide to what industries
should be expanded, contracted, or set up. They have suggested
instead that the degree of effective protection required by each industry provides the proper ranking of relative efficiency in terms
of comparative advantage.

We shall next examine these questions within the framework of
the standard general equilibrium model of international trade
theory, appropriately extended to cover intermediate goods.[1] The
advantages of this approach are felt to be the possibility of greater
clarification of the issues in the context of a simple explicit model
and also the integration of these interesting new policy problems
with traditional trade theory.

I

Assume that the economy is endowed with fixed supplies of two
primary factors: labor and capital. There are two final goods, X
and Y, and two intermediate goods, A and B. A fixed amount of A
and B per unit of each final good is required. The intermediate
goods are produced by labor and capital alone, each according to a
constant-returns-to-scale production function of the neoclassical
type. Labor and capital transform the fixed inputs of A and B into
the final goods X and Y, also according to conditions represented
by neoclassical production functions with constant returns to
scale. Thus labor and capital can be subsituted for each other in

---

[1]For other attempts at general equilibrium trade models incorporating tariffs on
intermediate goods see Corden (1969) and Ruffin (1969).

producing the final goods, but there are fixed coefficients for the inputs of the intermediate goods A and B into each of the final goods. A further assumption about the technology is that the strong factor-intensity assumption holds, meaning that at any given factor-price ratio the ranking of all four goods according to capital intensity remains unchanged.

Given the production functions for A and B and the requirements of each of these per unit of X and Y, we can distinguish net and gross production functions for X and Y as follows: The net production function for each of these goods shows the labor and capital combinations required to produce a unit of final output given the required inputs of A and B, while the gross production function shows the combinations of the two primary factors required to make a unit of final output as well as the required inputs of A and B. The relation between net and gross production for each good can be shown most conveniently in terms of isoquants. Select A and B isoquants such that the level of each indicates the amount required per unit of a final output, say X. These two isoquants can be combined with that for making one unit of X, given the inputs of A and B that are needed (as determined by the net production function) to form an isoquant showing labor-capital combinations required for producing a unit of X, inclusive of the inputs of A and B. This isoquant specifies the gross production function for X. The isoquants can be combined by inverting the isoquants for A and B and sliding them successively along the net isoquant for X as in Figure 9.1, so that the corner of the B isoquant diagram traces out the gross isoquant for one unit of X. The gross isoquant for Y is of course obtained in exactly the same way. The method of construction is such that the marginal rate of substitution between labor and capital is always equal in producing A,B, and X itself so that any labor-capital combination on the gross isoquant for X is efficient in the sense that less of either primary input must reduce the final output of X if the amount of the other primary input is held constant.

The isoquant maps corresponding to the gross production functions for X and Y, together with the fixed endowment of labor and

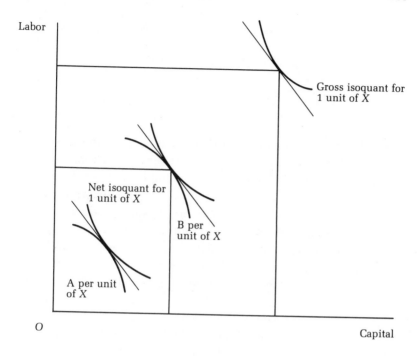

Figure 9.1

capital, make it possible to construct a box diagram and derive
from it a transformation curve. In a closed economy with perfect
competition, demand conditions will determine a point on the
transformation curve at which the economy produces. This will
correspond to a point on the efficiency locus of the box diagram,
which determines the factor-price ratio as the slope of the common tangent to the X and Y isoquants. The outputs of A and B are
determined by the output levels of X and Y and the fixed technical
coefficients relating input of A and B to output of X and Y. The
labor and capital allocated to A and B and to the "value adding"
activities transforming these intermediate goods into X and Y are
determined by the factor-price ratio, the production functions for
A and B, and the net production functions for X and Y.

The pricing relations in the model, following from the assumption of perfect competition, can be summarized as follows:

$$\frac{P_x}{P_y} = A_{ax}\frac{P_a}{P_y} + A_{bx}\frac{P_b}{P_y} + A_{lx}\frac{W}{P_y} + A_{kx}\frac{R}{P_y}$$

$$1 = A_{ay}\frac{P_a}{P_y} + A_{by}\frac{P_b}{P_y} + A_{ly}\frac{W}{P_y} + A_{ky}\frac{R}{P_y}$$

where the P's are commodity prices, W and R are the wage rate and capital rental, and the A_{ij}s are technical coefficients. All prices are expressed in terms of Y. Demand conditions determine P_x/P_y, and the corresponding factor-price ratio determines the capital-labor ratios and hence marginal physical productivities of labor and capital in the Y industry which are equal to W/P_y and R/P_y. The factor-price ratio also determines A_{lx}, A_{kx}, A_{ly} and A_{ky}. Since A_{ax}, A_{bx}, A_{ay} and A_{by} are fixed coefficients, this leaves only two unknowns, P_a/P_y and P_b/P_y, to be determined by the two equations.

Now that we have determined all price ratios in terms of Y the reciprocals of these price ratios will denote the quantities of A, B, and X that are each equal in value to one unit of Y—i.e., have the same factor cost. At this point it is necessary to distinguish between the price per unit of X and Y and the value added per unit of each of these commodities. Denoting the latter concept by $\overline{P}_x$ and $\overline{P}_y$ we have the relations

$$\overline{P}_x = P_x - A_{ax}\,P_a - A_{bx}P_b = \alpha P_x \quad 0 < \alpha < 1$$

$$\overline{P}_y = P_y - A_{ay}\,P_a - A_{bx}\,P_b = \beta P_y \quad 0 < \beta < 1$$

from which it is possible to find out the amount of value added in X and Y that is equal in value to 1 unit of Y. Thus suppose that $\alpha = \frac{2}{3}$ and $\beta = \frac{3}{4}$. This means that the value added on $1\frac{1}{3}$ units of Y is equal to the price of 1 unit of Y and that the value added on $1\frac{1}{2}$ units of X is equal to the price of a unit of X. If the price ratio is 2X:1Y, then the value added on 3 units of X is equal to the value added on $1\frac{1}{2}$ units of Y. If we also had, say, 5A and 4B being worth 1 unit of Y then we have the relation:

Value added on 3 units of X = value added on $1\frac{1}{3}$
units of Y = 5 units of A = 4 units of B.

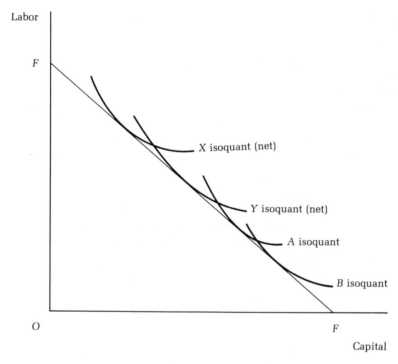

Figure 9.2

Since all these quantities have the same factor cost, we can use the Lerner diagram of Figure 9.2 to represent the situation; the slope of the factor cost line is determined in the manner explained previously. The relevant isoquants for X and Y correspond to the net production functions, since we are only taking value added. The strong factor-intensity assumption made earlier rules out the possibility of the isoquants intersecting more than once.

II

Suppose now that the economy has the opportunity to trade at fixed world prices for the different goods and that there are no tariffs, subsidies, or other interferences with free trade. This will of course have repercussions on the level of production in each of the four industries. These effects can be determined by reconstructing the Lerner diagram of Figure 9.2 in terms of world prices, which are now the only relevant ones. We shall again determine the amounts of A and B, and of value added in X and Y, that are equal in value (at world prices) to 1 unit of Y and hence equal to each other. Value added at world prices of X, for example, is determined by converting the value of 1 unit of X into terms of Y at the word price ratio and then subtracting the value of the fixed inputs of A and B required per unit of X in terms of Y, again at the world price ratios. Say that this value added at world prices per unit of X is worth $\frac{2}{5}$ unit of Y. Therefore, the value added on $2\frac{1}{2}$ units of X is worth 1Y at world prices. Similarly if the value added per unit of Y is worth $\frac{1}{2}$ Y at world prices then the value added on 2 units of Y is equal to 1Y at world prices and hence to the value added on $2\frac{1}{2}$ units of X. The prices of A and B in terms of Y at world prices present no problem of interpretation.

The Lerner diagram at world prices is shown in Figure 9.3. Again, the isoquants for X and Y correspond to the net production functions for those commodities. The configuration of the four isoquants is of course arbitrary, since no special assumption was made about the way in which the world prices differ from the equilibrium prices in the no-trade situation. All four commodities will be produced under free trade only in the exceptional circumstance in which all four isoquants have a common tangent; three will be produced only in the slightly less unlikely instance in which there exists a common tangent to any three (with the parallel tangent to the fourth isoquant located above the common tangent to the three, implying that production of this commodity is not worthwhile). The configuration depicted in Figure 9.3 is consistent with domestic production of only two goods, X and B, since with any other pair the cost of producing something of equivalent value at world prices is less in terms of domestic factor cost, and this opportunity is not taken up. The actual production levels of X and B will depend on the factor endowment of the economy. Some A must be imported, since X is produced within the country but A is not. Some Y will be imported. Either X or B or both will be exported, depending upon the relation between home demand and supply.

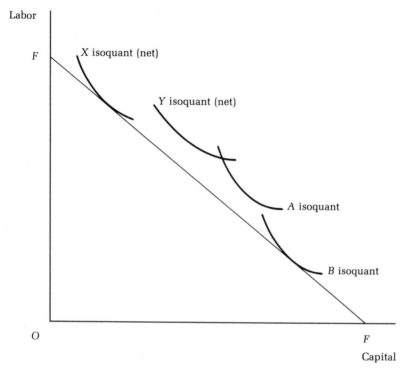

Figure 9.3

The effects of tariffs and subsidies can also be handled with the Lerner diagram. Domestic producers will allocate resources in response to the tariff or subsidy-inclusive world prices, which means that the pattern of specialization will be shifted. A tariff on an imported commodity raises its price so that fewer units of the commodity will be worth 1 unit of Y, which is our standard of account. If none of the goods were used as inputs then only the commodity on which a tariff or subsidy is imposed will have its isoquants shifted in the Lerner diagram. If tariffs are put on intermediate goods such as A or B, however, these will also affect X and Y, since value added at the tariff-inclusive world prices per unit of X and Y will be reduced. Thus it will require value added on more units of X and Y to be worth 1 unit of Y. The isoquants for A and B are therefore shifted inward when tariffs are imposed on these goods, but those for X and Y are shifted out. "Effective protection" for X and Y will be negative unless tariffs are imposed on X and Y to offset the higher costs of the intermediate inputs.

From Figure 9.3 it is possible to calculate the degree of protection required to induce domestic production of commodities Y and A. The percentage by which prices must be raised for these goods is determined by the excessive domestic cost of production, measured by the extent to which the tangents to the Y and A isoquants parallel to FF lie beyond FF itself. To leave the position of the X isoquant unchanged, however, requires that a tariff on X must also be imposed—one just sufficient to offset the effect of the tariff on A and so maintain zero effective protection.

III

It is now possible to appraise the Bruno-Krueger and Balassa-Schydlowsky approaches. If we call the price of a unit of Y one dollar of foreign exchange then the cost in terms of domestic resources of producing one dollar's worth of foreign exchange is given by the factor outlay line FF in Figure 9.3. The domestic resource cost per unit of foreign exchange is the same in sectors X and B, which are the only two industries viable under free trade; this is the minimum cost per unit of foreign exchange for the economy as a whole. The isoquants for A and Y also represent production worth one dollar of foreign exchange, but the domestic resource cost is higher in each case than the cost for X and B. The additional cost is measured by the extent to which a factor outlay line tangent to each of these isoquants and parallel to FF lies beyond FF. If we denote these percentages of additional cost R_a and R_y repectively, and the minimum cost for the economy as C^*, the domestic resource cost per unit of foreign exchange is $(1 + R_a)C^*$ in A, $(1 + R_y)C^*$ in Y, and C^* in X and B.

Domestic production of A and Y would become viable if sufficient protection is given to offset the excess costs of R_a and R_y. It is easily seen that the extent to which prices have to be raised—i.e., the rate of effective tariff protection—is equal to R_a and R_y. Hence ranking the industries according to the two criteria of the domestic resource cost per unit of foreign exchange and degree of effective protection required appear to come to the same thing and to be correct if conformity with static comparative advantage principles is accepted as the common objective of the two approaches.[2]

The first question that this conclusion raises is why Balassa and Schydlowsky felt the two criteria to be conflicting. The reason is that Bruno and Krueger classify inputs as either domestic or foreign, and in calculating domestic resource cost they take the direct and indirect primary inputs required for the domestic component of cost per unit. This means that for all inputs of intermediate goods we either accept all existing domestic industries supplying these items, regardless of efficiency, or that we already know which intermediate products can be produced efficiently at home and include only these items as domestic costs.

In the latter case it is easy to see that the same result as obtained above will hold. The isoquants for X and Y in the Lerner diagram will not correspond to the net production functions for these commodities (as in Figure 9.3) or to the gross production functions, but to a hybrid case where we have added to the direct requirements of primary inputs in the final stage only the primary inputs required for B, the domestically produced intermediate good, but not those required for A, which is available only through imports. The relevant prices for X and Y then become not just value added per unit but value added plus cost of the domestically produced intermediate good. Since this good is produced efficiently the two adjustments cancel each other out and so we get exactly the same result as in the previous section. However, this approach presupposes knowledge of the final result and so the procedure adopted here of working only with direct requirements of primary inputs appears superior.

Balassa and Schydlowsky, however, interpret Bruno and Krueger as accepting existing domestic production of intermediate goods, regardless of efficiency. It is then easy to show, as they

---

[2]This relationship is pointed out in Krueger (1972). In this paper, however, she is mainly concerned with situations in which she says the equivalence no longer applies.

do, that activities at later stages of production can be penalized by having inflated prices for their intermediate inputs. Thus suppose that X and B are the only industries viable under free trade and that A is the only intermediate input used to make X while B is the only one used to make Y. Suppose now that a tariff is put on A to induce domestic production of this commodity. Since A has now become a domestic good, we have to add the primary inputs needed to make the necessary amount of A input per unit of X output to the direct primary input requirements per unit of X. The domestic resource costs of making 1 unit of X are now higher, but foreign exchange earned (or saved) is also increased, since the A input required per unit of X is now no longer imported. The domestic resource cost per unit of foreign exchange in the integrated X industry is, however, higher than that in the original case when domestic production was confined to only the second stage, since the cost of producing the A component is higher than under free trade. The domestic resource cost per unit of foreign exchange earned or saved in the integrated Y industry is also above that of the free trade situation, since in the latter case production was confined to the efficient first stage only. If we compare the costs for the two integrated industries, it could well be that it is higher in the X industry than in the Y industry. The criterion therefore leads to a choice of an inefficient second stage industry over an efficient one, as a result of the tariff on A which makes it a domestic input. In terms of effective protection, however, it is clear that X has negative effective protection while Y has positive effective protection. The reason is that A, the input into X, has a tariff on it without there being any countervailing duty on the final output, whereas B, the input into Y, has no tariff and there is a tariff on the final output. Balassa and Schydlowsky therefore say that the effective protection criterion gives the right answer whereas the domestic resource cost criterion gives the wrong one.

From the analysis given earlier, however, it can be seen that if the domestic resource cost of the foreign exchange concept is applied to each activity or stage of production separately, it will

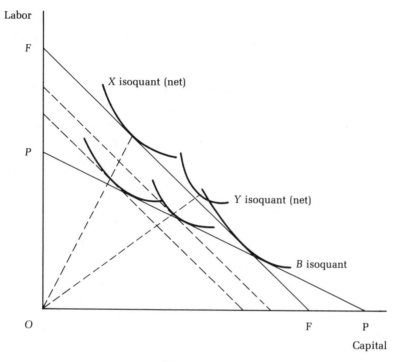

Figure 9.4

give the same result as effective protection. It is the practice of including indirect primary inputs that leads to the possibility pointed out by Balassa and Schydlowsky.

In the analysis so far it has been assumed that protection is imposed only to the minimum extent necessary to induce domestic production, so that the factor-price ratio remains the same as under free trade. In terms of Figure 9.3 this means imposing tariffs only to the extent necessary to shift the isoquants for the protected commodities inward until they become tangential to FF. Suppose, however, that protection of Y is carried further than this and we have the situation depicted in Figure 9.4. In this case the economy will again specialize only in two goods, which may be X and Y, or Y and B, depending upon the factor endowment of the economy.

It is assumed that the capital-labor ratio of the economy lies between the ratios for Y and B, so that these are the two goods that are produced. The factor-price ratio is indicated by the line PP.

The effect of the protection of Y has thus been to drive out the production of X, which can be efficiently produced under free trade. To make the X industry viable again, protection has to be given to it in sufficient degree to shift the X isoquant down until it is tangential to PP. The economy now produces X, Y, and B. The efficiency of these three industries can now be appraised in terms of the two criteria.

In terms of the effective protection criterion, B is clearly the most efficient, since it does not require any protection at all. It remains to compare the extent of protection in X and Y. Intuitively we would expect that the protection of X must be less, since it is efficient under free trade whereas Y is not. However, the opposite result is quite possible, as indicated in Figure 9.4. It is easy to see that the extent to which the X isoquant has to be shifted in from the free trade situation to tangency with PP may be greater than the extent to which the Y isoquant has to be shifted, in spite of the fact that it is initially tangential to FF whereas the isoquant for Y is not. The reason is that the factor-price ratio shifts in favor of labor as a result of protection, and X is more labor-intensive than Y. The unfavorable effect of the factor-price ratio shift can be strong enough to outweigh the initial advantage of X over Y at the free-trade factor prices.

The extent to which the X and Y isoquants are shifted in can be measured by drawing tangents parallel to FF and determining the extent to which these lie below FF. As drawn in Figure 9.4, the shift in the X isoquant is greater than in the Y isoquant, so that the degree of effective protection is greater for X than for Y, while it is zero for B. At the factor-price ratio represented by the slope of PP the three isoquants tangential to PP all have the same domestic resource cost. In terms of foreign exchange value, however, it is the three isoquants tangential to FF that are equivalent. Since the X isoquant is shifted in the most, it follows that the domestic resource cost per unit of foreign exchange is higher in X than in Y, while it is lowest in the *B* sector.[3] The two criteria again give the same ranking of the three industries. Since under free trade only the *X* and *B* industries will be efficient, it follows that neither criterion succeeds in ranking industries according to comparative advantage, as claimed by both groups of authors. Bruno, for instance, says of the domestic resource cost criterion that "it clearly measures comparative advantage" and Balassa and Schydlowsky say that "it would appear that if one adjusts for excess profits and disregards the possibility that labor unions have monopoly power in some industries, the ranking of industries by the effective rate of protection will provide an indication of static comparative advantage."[4] Both qualifications mentioned in the second quotation are not relevant to the present analysis, which assumes perfectly competitive pricing in all commodity and factor markets.

It is difficult to generalize as to how significant the difference in the rankings by the two criteria in the protection situation will be from the correct ranking at the free-trade factor-price ratio, because the authors do not report attempts to adjust their data to try to arrive at this ratio.[5] All corrections appear to be for the purpose of removing random or monopolistic deviations from "equilibrium" prices of the protection situation itself. Krueger performs a sensitivity analysis by changing the return on capital from 20 percent to 30 percent and reducing the real wage by 25 percent. She finds that the ranking of industries does not change. The differences in the individual figures, however, are not negligible, and with more disaggregation one cannot rule out the possibility of changes in ranking.

In any case the appeal of both approaches is that they propose relatively simple methods for finding out the true pattern of com-

---

[3]Alternatively we could measure the domestic resource cost per unit of foreign exchange by drawing tangents parallel to *PP* to each of the isoquants tangential to *FF* to obtain the same result.

[4]See Bruno (1967), p. 106 and Balassa and Schydlowsky (1968) p. 359.

[5]An interesting exercise along these lines is carried out in a study on tariffs in Southern African countries by Vernon Roningen, as part of his as yet unpublished doctoral dissertation at Columbia University.

parative advantage in economies that are extensively protected in one way or another. Requiring a knowledge of what the factor-price ratio would be in a hypothetical free-trade situation would meet the logical criticism pointed out here but at the price of raising formidable problems of empirical research.

V

In this discussion, no restriction has yet been placed on the way in which the fixed world prices under free trade differed from the prices in the no-trade situation. The Heckscher-Ohlin theory of comparative advantage, however, does assert that there is a relationship between the degree of capital (or labor) intensity in production of different goods and the pattern of comparative advantage. Given a list of goods ranked in order of capital intensity, the Heckscher-Ohlin theory predicts that export commodities would be at one end of the spectrum, noncompetitive imports at the other end, and competitive imports in between. There is a "chain of comparative advantage" with demand conditions determining the dividing line between exports and imports. If a given commodity is exported then all commodities that are more capital-intensive must be either exported or imported, but not both. This hypothesis in its strict interpretation depends upon identity of technology and demand patterns (further required to be "homothetic") in the trading countries. In the absence of these restrictions it is quite possible to break the systematic link between capital intensity and comparative advantage, as was done in the analysis here. It is interesting to discover, however, whether the Bruno-Krueger and Balassa-Schydlowsky criteria would provide a ranking in terms of comparative advantage if the Heckscher-Ohlin hypothesis is assumed to hold for the pattern of comparative advantage.

In Figure 9.5 the Lerner diagram is drawn so that the only two goods produced under free trade are at the labor-intensive end of the scale. A is exported and X is either exported or import-competing. Suppose now that it is desired to protect Y to such an extent that the factor-price ratio becomes the line PP instead of the

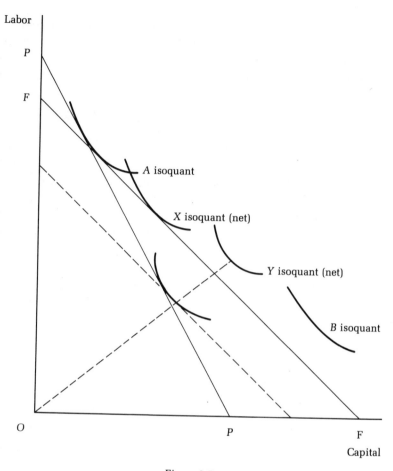

Figure 9.5

line FF. If no protection is given to X it will not be produced domestically. If X is accorded sufficient protection to shift its isoquant in until it becomes tangential to PP then there will be three sectors with positive output A, X, and Y. There is no protection for A and the rate of effective protection must be less for X than it is for Y. If domestic production of B is desired the rate of protection would have to be higher than for Y. It therefore follows that ranking industries by the degree of effective protection required also ranks them by comparative advantage. Similarly the domestic resource cost per unit of foreign exchange will give exactly the same ranking, since the extent to which each isoquant has to be shifted in until it is tangential to PP varies directly with the degree of capital intensity and thus the greater is the reduction in foreign exchange earned or saved.

It thus appears that the logical validity of the two approaches, which we have found to be equivalent under the assumption adopted, depends upon the extent to which the Heckscher-Ohlin hypothesis is relevant to the foreign trade of the country to which the analysis is applied. In practice it may turn out that useful results can be obtained even in the absence of this restriction, but this is a matter for extensive empirical investigation.

Thus far in our analysis, we have restricted the form of protection accorded domestic industries to the imposition of tariffs. Since world prices and tariff rates are both given exogenously, this simplifies the determination of internal price ratios considerably. If protection takes the form of fixed import quotas, however, the pattern of internal price ratios will depend upon the nature of demand and hence cannot be determined from knowledge of the world price ratios and the levels of the quotas alone. It is however true that, depending upon the nature of demand, a certain equilibrium set of internal price ratios will be determined, equating marginal rates of substitution in consumption with marginal rates of transformation in production. Given this set of prices the Lerner technique used in this paper will continue to apply as before. The same would hold true if we had a mixed system of both tariffs and quotas. What the deviation of domestic from world prices would now measure is not "effective tariffs" but "effective protection" due to either tariffs or quotas or both. All results obtained for the pure tariff case would hold unchanged if the form of protection were altered either to quotas or to a mixed system.

It also seems possible that the analysis could be extended to cover complications such as factor market distortions, but we shall not attempt to make such a determination here. What are really beyond the reach of the analysis undertaken here are such phenomena as increasing returns to scale, nonmalleability of capital, and monopoly. Extension to many periods does not need to cause undue difficulties so long as these factors are excluded. However, the main purpose of this chapter has been the somewhat negative one of pointing out that ranking industries by effective protection or domestic resource cost of foreign exchange does not necessarily rank them in terms of comparative advantage unless some rather strong further assumptions are made. If this result is valid for the simplified conditions assumed it is only likely to be strengthened if more complicating factors are assumed. In any case, once we leave the world of perfect competition the concepts of comparative advantage and economic efficiency themselves become somewhat hazy.

It is far from my intention to call into question the relevance and importance of the empirical results obtained in such studies as those of Bruno, Krueger, Lewis and Guisinger, and other similar exercises. I am only noting that more attention needs to be paid to the interpretation of these results in relation to the concept of comparative advantage.

Part Four

STRUCTURAL DISEQUILIBRIUM
Foreign Exchange Shortage and Relative Price Adjustment

CHAPTER 10

The "Foreign Exchange Gap" and Growth in Developing Economies

THE VIEW is now very widely held that the critical bottleneck restricting the rate of growth in the developing countries is the shortage of foreign exchange. The intellectual roots of this concept spread in many directions. The Latin-American structuralist school has long maintained that the "limited capacity to import" in relation to high and inelastic import requirements has been one of the main factors responsible for the chronic inflation and stagnation in that part of the world. The Indian strategy of development as exemplified in the second Five Year Plan inspired by theories of P. C. Mahalanobis (based on the assumption of a closed economy) also encountered the foreign exchange bottleneck as import requirements for new capital goods industries outran the earnings available from stagnant export sectors. Finally there has been the influence of the programming models of Chenery and his various associates, which have apparently identified foreign exchange as being the effective binding constraint for many countries. All of these diverse influences have crystalized in the UNCTAD conferences, where the doctrine of the foreign exchange constraint has been developed and institutionalized in the Secretariat, under the leadership of Raul Prebisch.

While this view has come to be widely held in "development" circles, it appears that there is not much sympathy for it among the majority of professional economists, whose natural reaction on being told that there is a shortage of something is to feel that this must be caused by interferences with the free play of the price mechanism—in this case by governments in the market for foreign exchange.

In this chapter we shall attempt to examine the foreign exchange constraint doctrine from the standpoint of the pure theory of international trade. We hope to be able to identify precisely the assumptions on which it depends and the manner in which it might restrict the growth rates attainable in developing economies.[1]

I

In terms of conventional economic theory, the fundamental constraint on growth is the willingness to save. Given the productivity of capital, the greater the willingness of a society to save—that is, to restrain its consumption—the greater will be the growth of its total product. It is, however, asserted that in some cases developing economies may be in a situation where raising the rate of saving will have no effect on the rate of growth, which is taken as being determined by the availability of foreign exchange.

The possibility of this can be shown by means of the following simple model. Suppose that a country produces a single commodity, which can be used for consumption, investment, or export. Imports obtainable at a fixed price in terms of exports are needed only for investment in fixed proportions with domestic output. Production of domestic output is a function of the stock of capital alone. The working of the model is best explained in Figure 10. 1.

The distance *OU* measures the maximum attainable level of domestic production with the initial capital stock. With a given propensity to consume, a distance *OR* can be marked off, denoting

---

[1] The main references are Chenery and Bruno (1962), Chenery and Strout (1966), McKinnon (1964), Linder (1967) and Bhagwati (1966).

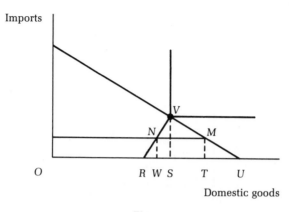

Figure 10.1

the amount of domestic output consumed. The slope of *UV* indicates the terms of trade. A family of L-shaped isoquants for investment goods output can be drawn with the origin at *R*, the
slope of the line through *R* indicating the proportions in which
domestic and imported inputs are used in investment. The maximum level of investment is measured by *RV* and domestic output
is divided between *OR* of consumption, *RS* of investment, and *SU*
of exports—which is exchanged for *VS* of imports. The lower the
propensity to consume, the closer will *R* be to the origin and the
larger, therefore, will be the level of investment, and (with a given
capital-output ratio) the higher the rate of growth.

Suppose, however, that the economy is only able to export *UT*
or, alternatively, that *MT* is the maximum level of imports obtainable regardless of the level of exports. In this case the maximum
level of investment obtainable is measured by *RN*, and *WT* of
domestic output will be redundant since only *RW* is required for
investment and only *TU* need or can be exported. The "foreign
exchange gap" will be measured by the difference between *VS*
and *MT*. Under these circumstances, reducing the propensity to
consume will not raise investment at all but will simply increase
the amount of domestic output that is redundant.

The situation can also be represented in terms of a diagram
showing the tradeoff between consumption and investment as in

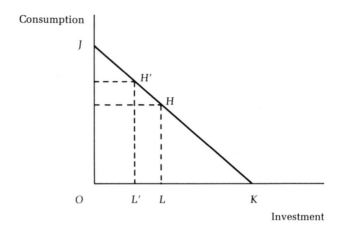

Figure 10.2

Figure 10. 2. The cost of a unit of investment in terms of domestic goods can be obtained by adding the direct input of these goods required per unit of investment to the imported input required, the latter being valued at the fixed terms of trade. If all domestic output is used for consumption, then *OJ* will be the maximum available, and with no constraints on trade, society could transform *OJ* of consumption into a maximum of *OK* investment. Let *HL* and *OL* indicate the levels of consumption and investment that would be chosen in the absence of constraints on trade. If a constraint on trade existed such that *OL'* was the maximum feasible level of investment, then reducing consumption below *H'L'* would have no effect on investment and growth, since the marginal domestic resources freed would not be transformable into imports that are essential for investment. This is the sense in which it is asserted that the willingness to save and invest on the part of the developing countries is frustrated by the foreign exchange constraint.

Several policy implications have been drawn from this analysis. One is the need for export promotion or import substitution in the

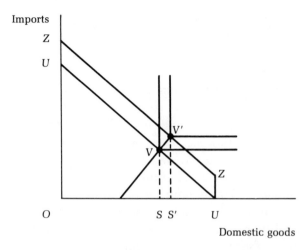

Figure 10.3

development strategy of the country itself. Another is the need for
a reduction in the obstacles to trade expansion placed in the way
of the developing countries' efforts to penetrate the markets of developed countries. In addition there is the argument that foreign
aid will be more productive under these circumstances than in the
case in which a more conventional shortage of saving is at the
basis of the failure of developing countries to grow more rapidly.

This last point can be illustrated in Figure 10.3. With no trade
constraint, the maximum level of investment with a given propensity to consume and no foreign aid will be indicated by the point
V. If foreign aid of UZ is given, the maximum level of investment
will be shifted to V'. Observe that imports do not rise by the full
amount of the foreign aid, since exports are reduced by SS' in
order to release complementary domestic inputs for investment.
In the case in which the foreign exchange constraint is binding,
instead of the saving constraint, there will be redundant domestic
output. This means that imports for investment purposes can
increase by the full amount of the foreign aid. The growth-
promoting effect of foreign aid is thus higher in the latter in-

stance.[2] In terms of Figure 10.3, V' will be directly above V and
SS' will come out of consumption instead of exports.

The simple model that we have been discussing appears to
elucidate the main propositions of the theory of foreign exchange
constraint, stripped of the details of the elaborate programming
models in which they are usually embedded. The general accept-
ability of these conclusions will naturally depend on the plausi-
bility of the assumptions. It is easy to see that the analysis
depends to a critical degree, on the impossibility of substituting
domestic for imported inputs into the production of the investment goods sector. The assumption of rigidly fixed technical coefficients may be valid in each particular line of investment, but the
overall proportions can be changed by varying the composition of
investment so that the model assumes that not only techniques
but also demand patterns are rigidly determined. The model as
presented here assumes that imported goods are not required for
consumption purposes, although it would make no difference if a
fixed requirement of imports for comsumption was also assumed.

II

Next, we shall add consumption of imported goods to the model.
The proportion of imported and domestic goods consumed will
depend on relative prices. This extension of the model to handle
a choice between imported and domestic consumer goods is easily accomplished by an adaption of the basic diagram of the first
section. In Figure 10.4 let OU represent the maximum level of
domestic production and the slope of UU' the terms of trade.
Given the propensity to save, the line RR', indicating the

---

[2] This result assumes fixed values of all the relevant parameters. In private correspondence J. Vanek has pointed out that if the marginal propensity to save is
greater than the average, a process of growth with foreign aid to ease a savings gap
will eventually become self-sustaining, whereas there is no such automatic mechanism for aid given to ease a foreign exchange gap to become self-liquidating unless
specific policies are pursued to that end.

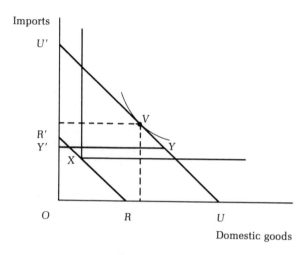

Figure 10.4

resources available for investment, can be determined. The point X, where the family of L-shaped isoquants is tangential to RR', determines the imported and domestic inputs into investment and also serves as the origin for a family of consumption indifference curves. It is convenient (though not strictly necessary for all the results that follow) to assume that these curves are "homothetic." The point V, where the indifference curve system is tangential to UU', represents the equilibrium point for the economy as a whole in the absence of any constraints on trade. The higher the propensity to save the higher will be the output of investment goods and the rate of growth.

As before, we can imagine that there is a restriction on trade so that $OUYY'$ instead of OUU' becomes the feasible set. The effect of this on growth depends upon whether consumption or investment bears the burden of the reduced opportunities available. In Figure 10.4, it would be possible to maintain the level of investment by switching consumption from V to Y, but since Y could well be below the point on UU' where it is cut by the investment isoquant through X, it is conceivable that there is no reduction in consumption that will allow the desired investment level to be maintained. Thus the foreign exchange constraint doctrine would appear to be valid even when there is a choice between imported and domestic consumption.

This conclusion, however, requires further examination. First, we need to be more specific about the constraint on trade. If the limitation is caused by internal factors restricting the supply of exports, the implication is obviously that these should be removed. To be relevant the restriction must be one that, because of conditions in foreign markets, is beyond the control of the domestic authorities. Suppose that world demand is such that the country can export and import at fixed terms up to the point Y but that beyond that point increasing exports result in a constant supply of imports. In other words the demand for exports has unitary elasticity beyond the point Y. The offer curve of the rest of the world is, therefore, UYY'.

The equilibrium terms of trade and export-import volumes can be determined by constructing a domestic offer curve to match against the foreign offer curve UYY'. The terms of trade can be varied by rotating UU' on U. Given the propensity to save, the resources available for investment at each value of the terms of trade can be obtained by rotating RR' on R, parallel to the rotation of UU' on U. At each value of the terms of trade, the tangency of the investment isoquants with RR' will give the imported and domestic inputs required for investment as well as the origin for placing the consumption-indifference map to determine the overall pattern of demand for imported and domestic goods by tangency with the parellel UU'. The locus of all these points form the domestic offer curve UVV' in Figure 10.5.

The equilibrium terms of trade will be measured by the slope of UZ where Z is the point of intersection of the domestic and foreign offer curves. The point Z will obviously be inferior to point V, but it should be noted that V is essentially irrelevant to the problem facing the country. It only plays a role if it is assumed that any desired volume of trade can take place at terms equal to the slope of UU', in which case it would represent the equilibrium point. The foreign exchange gap analysis starts by calculating foreign exchange required at too favorable terms and thus arrives at a gap by deducting foreign exchange actually available. At the

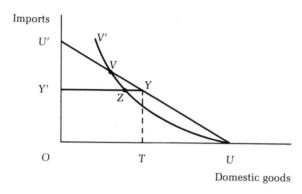

Figure 10.5

equilibrium terms of trade UZ requirements and availabilities are exactly matched and there is no gap.

As one moves along the domestic offer curve from U to V', the rate of growth will be rising. The fixed propensity to save means that the value of investment in terms of domestic goods is the same all along the offer curve, but since the cost of a unit of investment goods in terms of domestic goods is lower, the more favorable the terms of trade, the greater will be the increment of capital in real terms and hence the higher the rate of growth as one moves along the domestic offer curve from U to V'. The growth rate of the economy will, therefore, be lower at Z than at V.

The free trade equilibrium point Z, however, is clearly not an optimum point, since the point Y—which is also on the foreign offer curve—would give the same amount of foreign goods for the exchange of fewer domestic goods. A centrally planned economy, for example, could export UT of domestic goods and import TY of foreign goods. These imports and the remaining OT of domestic goods could then be allocated through the price mechanism, with the relative price of the goods changing until equilibrium is established. The socially desired propensity to save can be introduced by allocating to the investment sector the appropriate fraction of national income, evaluated by applying the price ratio at each round of the trial-and-error process to the combination of OT domestic goods and YT imports.

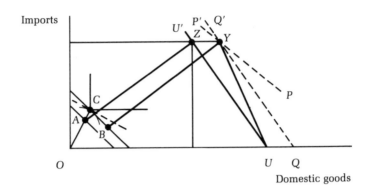

Figure 10.6

Alternatively, the state could impose a tariff and redistribute the proceeds in such a way that the domestic offer curve is shrunk in to intersect the foreign offer curve at Y instead of Z. In either case, the slope of the line PP' through Y in Figure 10.6 could represent the equilibrium internal price ratio between the two goods, representing a premium on foreign goods as compared with the external terms of trade represented by the slope of UU'.

The rate of growth of the economy will be higher at Y than at Z. Since the internal relative price of imports is higher at Y than at Z, this statement requires some proof, which is provided in Figure 10.6. The points Z and Y in Figure 10.5 in effect determine two "boxes" of commodity availabilities, which are shown in Figure 10.6. The origin of the consumption-indifference map can be placed at the northeast corner of the boxes instead of at the tangency point of the investment isoquants, as in the usual box diagram analysis. Let A be the original equilibrium point inside the box diagram, corresponding to Z. As a result of making the optimal trade restriction either through state control or tariff policy, the point Y becomes attainable with more domestic goods and the same amount of imports. Suppose that the same internal price ratio were to prevail at Y as at Z (this is indicated by QQ' through Y having the same slope as UU' through Z). With the same propensity to save, C would now represent the equilibrium point for investment goods and B for consumption. Clearly there is an excess demand for imports and an excess supply of domestic goods. The relative price of imports therefore has to be raised. This will increase national income measured in terms of the domestic good and also raise proportionately the value of investment in terms of domestic goods, since the propensity to save is fixed. The fraction of imports allocated to investment, however, remains the same as at C, since by virtue of the fixed propensity to save, pivoting the relative price line on Y implies pivoting it in parallel fashion on C. In equilibrium the relative price line will have the slope of PP', and the line through C parallel to PP' will be tangential to a consumption indifference curve at C. Investment is therefore larger, and with the same production of domestic goods the rate of growth corresponding to Y will be higher than that corresponding to Z. Consumers, however, will have fewer imports at Y than at Z although they will have more domestic goods to compensate for this.

The way Figure 10.6 is drawn assumes that the investment goods sector has a higher ratio of imported to domestic goods at the same price ratio than consumption, but the results will still hold in the opposite case as well.

The analysis has so far assumed a fixed propensity to save. The effect of a change in this propensity on the rate of growth can readily be ascertained for both the free trade and optimal trade cases. The free trade case is analyzed first in Figure 10.7. In this diagram UT and ZT are the volumes of exports and imports respectively, and the slope of UZ measures the terms of trade in free trade equilibrium. Here RR' is the line denoting the value of resources devoted to investment corresponding to the original propensity to save. If one takes Z as the origin for the consumption-indifference map, A is the original equilibrium position where an investment isoquant and a consumption indifference curve are tangential to each other. Suppose now that there is an increase in the propensity to save such that the investment line is shifted from RR' to SS'. The investment equilibrium point shifts to B and the consumption equilibrium point to C, which results in an excess demand for imports of CD and an excess supply of domestic goods of BD. The terms of trade will thus move adversely for the

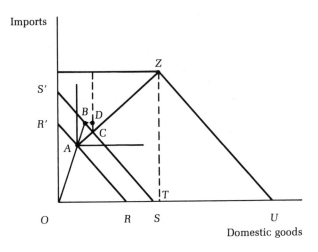

Figure 10.7

country, which will result in an exchange of more exports for the same amount of imports. This means that the investment line will swing to the left with the point S remaining fixed, which will have the effect of reducing investment below the level attained at B. The question is whether it is possible for this to reverse completely the increase in the propensity to save. The adverse shift in the terms of trade must result in a reduction in consumption demand for imports (since imports are not inferior goods by hypothesis) and so the new equilibrium position must be somewhere on OAB above the point C. But since C is already above A, we see that the terms of trade shift cannot reverse the expansion of investment completely. Thus the greater the propensity to save, the greater the rate of growth. If consumption were more import intensive than investment, an increase in the propensity to save would improve the terms of trade, thus increasing investment even more in this case.

In the optimal trade situation, the same results will follow except that the availability of each good will be the same before and after the change in the propensity to save, since it is only the internal and not the external price ratio that will be affected by the change in demand.

III

In the model just described, we have shown how the equilibrium terms of trade and rate of growth are determined, given the propensity to save. No foreign exchange gap appeared, since the relative prices of domestic and foreign goods adjust to clear any disequilibrium in the foreign exchange market. This conclusion requires reconciliation with the contention that the nature of the foreign exchange gap in developing countries is a situation that no amount of relative price adjustment can alleviate, with the result that the only solution is the provision of the requisite amount of foreign aid. Jaroslav Vanek, for example, has recently expressed this point of view.[3]

The difference between our formulation and his is that he takes the rate of growth as given once and for all, so that variation in the relative price of foreign and domestic goods has no effect on the foreign exchange required for investment, since fixed proportions of the two types of inputs is of course assumed. With a ceiling imposed on foreign exchange earnings also by hypothesis, we have a situation where both the demand and supply for foreign exchange are perfectly inelastic, with the former exceeding the latter to produce the gap that has to be filled by aid.

It is clear, however, that the postulated conditions cannot hold in any actual market situation. As the terms of trade shift adversely, the real income of the country is reduced, and the maintenance of a fixed investment program implies that the propensity to save is rising. If the fixed-gap theory is interpreted literally, it would imply that the propensity to save can increase to 100 percent and even beyond! What is perfectly correct and reasonable is to point out that if a certain "required" rate of growth is postulated, and the trading conditions facing the country and the propensity to save are also taken as being given, then the required growth rate may not be attainable without foreign assistance. In the absence of such assistance, the growth rate will be reduced to conformity with the other conditions through the adjustment of relative foreign and domestic prices. The price adjustment wipes out the

[3] See Vanek (1967), chapter 6.

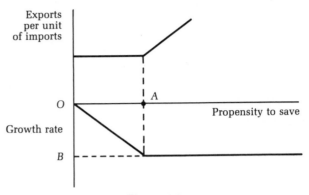

Figure 10.8

gap by reducing both consumption and investment demand for imports. Thus when critics of the gap theory assert that the so-called gap is only the manifestation of an overvalued currency and when proponents of the theory assert that it is a fundamental "structural" phenomenon, both are in a sense right; while relative price adjustment can close the gap, it cannot do so in a way that leaves the growth rate at the original level.

The question that now arises is whether the postulated growth rate can be attained without foreign aid if there is an increase in the propensity to save, while trading opportunities remain the same. To answer the question, let us consider the foreign offer curve UYY' in the diagrams of the previous section. Assume first that imports are required only for investment. With a zero propensity to save, there will of course be no trade and no growth. Increasing the propensity to save will lead to increasing trade volumes. In addition, the rate of growth will increase in the same proportion as the propensity to save, since the terms of trade will be constant along the segment UY of the foreign offer curve. Raising the propensity to save beyond the point where the investment isoquant is tangential to UYY' at Y, however, leads to a worsening of the terms of trade, while it leaves the rate of growth—measured in terms of the domestic good—unchanged. The relationship between the saving rate, terms of trade, and the growth rate is depicted in Figure 10.8.

Figure 10.8 shows that OA is the maximum effective propensity

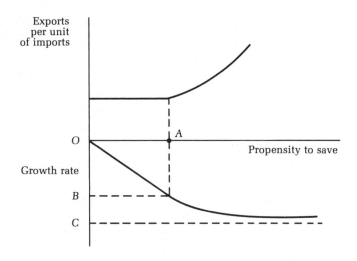

Figure 10.9

to save. Going beyond that leaves the growth rate unchanged and is also "immiserizing," since it reduces consumption as well. If the required growth rate is less than *OB* it will be obtainable without foreign assistance, provided that the propensity to save is sufficiently high. If the propensity to save is not sufficiently high, there is a "saving gap." In such a case the role of foreign assistance is to supplement the inadequate domestic saving. If the desired growth rate is greater than *OB* it is impossible for the country to attain that rate without foreign assistance, whatever the level of its propensity to save. Growth in this case is limited by the shortage of foreign exchange in relation to the import requirements of investment.

If one now supposes that imports are required for consumption as well, then the analysis of section II for the free-trade case indicates that the diagram corresponding to Figure 10.8 will be as shown in Figure 10.9.

The difference from Figure 10.8 is that the growth rate continues to increase as the propensity to save is increased, but it cannot go beyond the level *OC*, which is the growth rate corresponding to a propensity to save of 100 percent. Thus, unlike the case of Figure 10.8 beyond the level *OA*, increases in the propensity to save are never useless from the point of view of increasing the growth rate, but the marginal effectiveness is nevertheless diminishing.

Growth rates higher than OC are impossible to attain without foreign assistance. The effect of introducing imports of consumption is thus to extend the growth rates attainable in the absence of foreign assistance from OB to OC. Of course, in practice, there will be a limit to the extent to which the propensity to save can be raised so that foreign assistance will be necessary for growth rates lower than OC or even perhaps OB.

Raising the propensity to save beyond OA in this model will make the country worse off generally (since more exports of domestic goods have to be given for the same volume of total imports) but this increase nevertheless has a favorable effect on growth because it releases more imports for investment than for consumption. If there is government intervention to maintain a constant level of exports (the optimal trade case) then the overall availabilities of commodities will remain the same, but an increasing amount of each will be diverted to investment. The change in relative prices will be purely internal, as the external terms of trade will be fixed.

Throughout we have been assuming fixed coefficients in investment. Suppose, however, that imported and domestic inputs could be substituted continuously for each other as in a neoclassical production function, but that investment would remain more import intensive than consumption. To get even closer to conventional trade theory, let us also assume that the foreign offer curve has the usual convex slope instead of being composed of two linear segments. The anlysis of Section II can also be applied readily to this model, and a diagram corresponding to Figures 10.8 and 10.9 obtained. It is obvious that the only difference from Figure 10.8 would be that the linear segments of each curve up to OA would disappear so that we have a smoothly convex curve in each panel of the diagram.

The foreign exchange constraint doctrine has been interpreted here as a ceiling on foreign exchange earnings. It is possible to go further and assert that the foreign offer curve turns downward instead of just flattening out so that more exports result in less imports rather than the same amount. Under these circumstances raising the rate of saving could result in lowering the rate of growth after a point. While foreign demand for exports could well be inelastic for particular countries and commodities—such as coffee from Brazil—it is perhaps rather implausible to expect such a relation to hold for exports as a whole, unless there is some reason for the reduction in consumption to be concentrated heavily on nontradable goods. If such a condition were to hold, however, it then follows that there would again be a limit on the effective rate of saving.

Taking the opposite extreme, critics of the gap doctrine frequently point to the experience of Hong Kong and Taiwan for example, in attaining very high rates of export growth. Against this view it can be argued that such "export miracles" are possible only for some small economies so that the doctrine is interpreted to hold for the developing world as a whole and not for every individual country. Such conditions would appear to be likely, since labor-intensive manufactures have usually been the goods involved, and developed nations appear to be very sensitive to having their markets penetrated in this sphere.[4]

IV

Our analysis has attempted to show that the implication derived from the "foreign exchange gap" theory (that increases in the propensity to save may have no effect in raising the rate of growth in less developed countries) is not valid if there are imports for consumption as well as investment. What is true, even under much weaker assumptions about the technology of investment and trading opportunities, is that attempting to raise the rate of growth in a developing country by increasing the propensity to save can run into diminishing returns through worsening terms of trade if investment is more import-intensive than consumption.

---

[4] In this connection see the interesting exchange between Myint and Urquidi in Samuelson (1969).

More saving is never redundant but it can become increasingly less effective in raising the rate of growth while of course becoming increasingly costly in terms of consumption foregone. If foreign demand for exports is of less than unit elasticity, it is possible for increased saving to reduce the rate of growth.

The formulation of the problem in more familiar terms would appear to be more satisfactory, since it can include the usual "gap" model as a special case while retaining the main point of the argument: that limited trading opportunities restrict the growth that less developed countries can attain through their unaided efforts alone.

CHAPTER 11

A "Structuralist" Model of Inflation, Devaluation, and Stabilization

THE LONG experience of persistent inflation in several Latin-American countries has given rise to a protracted controversy in the region between the so-called "monetarist" and "structuralist" interpretations of this experience.[1] The more conventional monetarist view asserts that inflation has simply been the result of excess demand generated by irresponsible monetary expansion. The structuralist position, on the other hand, has maintained that inflation has been the product of more fundamental and deep-seated forces inherent in the nature of the economic systems of the Latin American countries: a chronic shortage of foreign exchange, inelastic food supply, powerful industrial trade unions, and so on. The policy implications of the alternative theories are also widely divergent. The monetarist approach recommends the classic devices for curbing excess demand and balance of payments deficits, monetary restriction, and exchange depreciation. The structuralists insist that such measures will only result in the aggravation of the problem of inflation, unless a socially unacceptable degree of unemployment is created, which can only be maintained for a short time, after which the underly-

---

[1] See Baer and Kerstenetsky (1964) for extensive discussion and references. An important further contribution in the structuralist tradition is Olivera (1964).

ing structural factors will again bring about the return of inflation. The structuralists are not, however, very clear on what alternative policies they would propose.

The monetarist position has an advantage: a simple, elegant, and rigorous theory is available as an intellectual tool in the form of the neo-Quantity Theory. This theory may be used to "explain" inflation in the usual regression sense by changes in the quantity of money and a demand for real balances function, which depends on the rate of inflation itself. The model that Cagan (1956) first used in his classic study of seven European hyperinflations has been applied to Chile, for example, with very successful statistical results.

The structuralists, on the other hand, do not appear to have been able to formulate a precise model from which they are able to deduce the propositions that they advance about inflation and stabilization from a minimum set of mutually consistent postulates. In this chapter we shall try to formulate such a model in very simple terms and to examine the controversy in the light of it.

The approach that we shall use is a model of internal and external balance that has been developed by a number of economists connected at one time or another with the Australian National University such as T. W. Swan, W. G. Salter, W. M. Corden, and I. F. Pearce.[2] This model has been previously used in a Latin American context by C. F. Diaz Alejandro (1965) in his study of Argentine devaluation. He did not, however, fully exploit its potentialities as a tool for the analysis of inflation. Arnold Harberger has also used a similar model independently in his contribution to the volume edited by Baer and Kerstenetsky (1964).

I

We shall begin by dividing the economy into two sectors, one producing "traded" and the other "domestic" goods. We shall include in the first category all exportables as well as all importables that can enter the country either freely or at nonprohibi-

[2] See Corden (1960) for the most detailed exposition of this model and references to the Australian tradition.

tive tariff rates. We shall include in the second category not only the standard instances of nontraded goods such as services, public utilities, and so on but also goods that might have been imported but are not, because of prohibitive tariffs or restrictive quotas. When combined with the "small country" assumption that prices of traded goods are determined independently of local demand and supply, this assumption results in the fact that the price level of traded goods is determined by world prices and local tariff rates—assumed given—and the rate of exchange—which will be either a variable or a policy parameter in the analysis. The price level of domestic goods, on the other hand, is taken to be determined on a markup basis and hence depends critically on the level of money wage rates. It is assumed that the domestic goods sector is quite sizable, built up by the usual type of import substitution policies, as in countries such as Argentina and Brazil. The labor force in this sector is taken to be organized into strong trade unions, which can bargain for higher money wage rates in response to changes in the cost of living. Traded goods are assumed to form an important part of the workers' budget.

Given the economy's endowment of labor, capital, and natural resources, and the technology of production, there will be a production-possibilities curve such as *PP* in Figure 11.1. Demand patterns will determine an equilibrium point on *PP* such as *Q*, at which the production and consumption of each type of good is equal and hence the balance of trade is zero. The slope of the tangent to *PP* at *Q*, denoted *DD*, determines the relative prices of traded and domestic goods or "real exchange rate," as we have called it in chapter 6, that are consistent with equilibrium. We can write this equilibrium price ratio as

$$\pi = \frac{P_T R}{P_D}$$

With π fixed by the "real" part of the system, equilibrium is consistent with any values of P_T, the given world prices adjusted for any tariffs and subsidies; P_D, the nominal price level of domestic goods; and R, the exchange rate that satisfies the above equation.

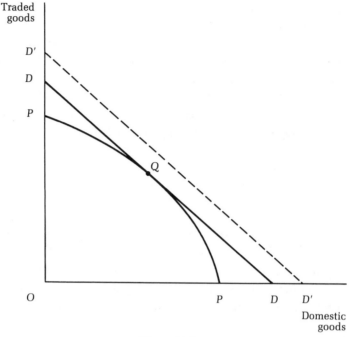

Figure 11.1

The model can now be applied to the analysis of inflation. We shall first use it to illustrate the conventional monetarist or "excess demand" theory of inflation and then proceed to the more important task of providing an interpretation of the structuralist approach.

Suppose that as a result of deficit financing by the government or excessive credit creation by private banks money incomes in the economy increase. At constant prices let the expanded money income be as indicated by $D'D'$ in Figure 11.1. If there is a freely floating exchange rate regime, then the effect of the excess demand will be to raise the prices of both traded and domestic goods. Real income will therefore shrink, $D'D'$ is shifted in until it coincides with DD, and the equilibrium position of the real sector will be restored, with the price levels in the two sectors raised in the same proportion. Continuous expansion of demand will

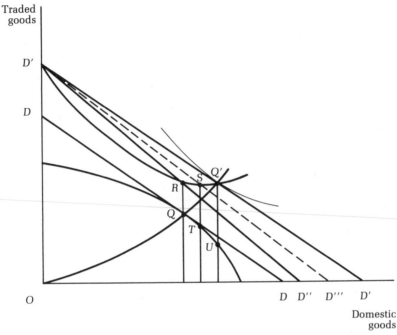

Figure 11.2

create continuous inflation, but under the conditions assumed there will be no effect on the real part of the system. Inflation could be brought to an end by simply refraining from further monetary expansion at absolute price levels and money income that are just sufficient to maintain the economy at Q. Inflation in this case is merely the product of macroeconomic mis-management. The process might be generated or reinforced by ris-ing money wages, but this can only operate to the extent that the authorities follow a permissive monetary policy.

In the case of fixed exchange rates things are more complicated, since monetary expansion will have repercussions on relative prices, production, and consumption. In Figure 11.2, $D'D'$ again represents the expansion of money income at constant prices (rel-ative and absolute). The demand for traded goods at Q' on $D'D'$ can be satisfied, assuming that foreign exchange reserves or international credit is available. There will, however, be an excess demand for domestic goods in the short run, the production of which will initially be confined to the supply corresponding to point Q on DD. This will cause a rise in the price of domestic goods, which will continue until demand is equal to the initial supply. Real income will decline to D'D'' and the equilibrium point in the short run will be at R. The deficit in the balance of payments will be measured by QR. If we are willing to represent the preferences of the community by a system of indifference curves, R will be the point on the price-consumption curve —generated by varying the price of domestic goods—vertically above Q.

Relative prices and marginal costs of production are, however, out of line, which will cause a shift of resources toward domestic goods. Their price will be lowered and hence real income will be raised. The budget line for the economy shifts out to D'D'''; consumers will be in equilibrium at the point S on the price-con-sumption curve D'RSQ', while producers will be in equilibrium at the point T vertically below on the transformation curve. The equilibrium points S and T at which relative prices are equal to marginal rates of substitution in consumption and production re-spectively—must exist, since at the point Q the relative price slope is steeper than the slope of the transformation curve whereas at the point U directly below Q' the reverse must be the case since the slope of the transformation curve at Q is equal to the slope of the tangent at Q'. There must therefore be a point in be-tween at which the slope of the budget line intersecting the price-consumption curve is equal to the slope of the transformation curve at the point vertically below. The import surplus in equilib-rium is measured by the distance ST.

The difference that the fixed exchange rate regime makes is that the inflation caused by the creation of excess demand produces significant real effects. The composition of production is shifted toward domestic goods and a permanent trade deficit emerges. Inflation with a fixed exchange rate is thus a potent force for the creation of a lopsided economic structure and an economy plagued with chronic balance of payments difficulties. In this

model the common structuralist argument that inflation is somehow the result of a preexisting foreign exchange shortage clearly
inverts the casual sequence. The policy recommendation flowing
from the model is simple. Both inflation and the balance of
payments deficit would be cured by deflation or devaluation, furthermore, these classical remedies will not result in unemployment, since full employment and balance of payments equilibrium can be achieved at a lower level of aggregate demand.

II

We shall now examine structuralist arguments in the context of
the same model used in the previous section. A fixed-exchange-
rate regime is assumed. Even if we start in a position of equilibrium (with full employment, balanced trade, and relative prices
equal to marginal rates of substitution in consumption and
production) it is unlikely that economic growth could proceed in
so balanced a fashion that equilibrium would continue to be
preserved at the same relative prices. If relative prices do not
change we can expect excess demand to develop in one market
and hence excess supply in the other. Following the structuralist
point about a chronic tendency to foreign exchange shortage, we
shall assume that excess demand emerges for traded goods and
hence excess supply for domestic goods. In Figure 11.3 the level
of total expenditure is indicated by DD', the slope of which
measures the existing relative prices. The production point is Q
and the consumption point is Q'. Thus while there is macroeconomic balance in the demand and supply of goods there is structural imbalance due to the fact that the patterns of production and
consumption at this level of income and expenditure do not mesh.
What is required is a realignment of relative prices, involoving a
decline in the relative price of domestic goods, to attain full equilibrium at Q.''

The important question that arises is how this relative price adjustment is to be brought about. Suppose that prices in the domestic goods sector are inflexible downward. This means that the adjustment can only be brought about by a depreciation of the

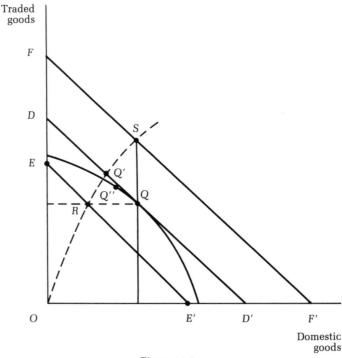

Figure 11.3

exchange rate, which the government, for the usual reasons, might not be willing to do. If aggregate demand is preserved at DD' there will be a deficit in the balance of trade and accumulation of unsold stocks in the domestic goods sector. This means that production in this sector will be cut back, unemployment will be created, and incomes will fall. If the government remains passive this process will continue until the point R is reached on the income-consumption path OQ' . At this point total expenditure has shrunk to EE', foreign trade is balanced, and so is the demand and supply of domestic goods.

The question arises as to whether the unemployed resources in the domestic goods sector would not move into the traded goods sector, lowering wages there and thus increasing profits. They would thereby induce an expansion of production of traded goods and the general level of income, which would generate secondary rounds of expenditure on domestic goods as well until the unemployment were eliminated. To this the structuralist answer would presumably be that there is very low mobility of labor from the domestic to the traded sector, particularly if the former is largely concentrated in urban areas and the latter in rural areas. Furthermore wages in the traded goods sector may also be inflexible downward, so that the traded goods sector receives insufficient inducement to expand. Given sufficient time a reallocation of resources could undoubtedly be brought about, but it might nevertheless be reasonably maintained that a serious depression might exist for some time before the readjustment is complete.

If the government is not willing either to devalue its currency or to allow substantial unemployment to emerge it has a third alternative: to expand income by fiscal or monetary policy to FF', so that at unchanged relative prices the demand for domestic goods is equal to the supply at the full employment point Q. The price of this, however, is the expansion of the trade deficit to SQ. The government has thus deliberately created excess demand (measured by the extent to which FF' lies outside DD') to prevent the emergence of structural unemployment. This policy will require continuous injection of money—say through a budget deficit—by an amount equal to the balance of payments deficit, so that the money supply remains constant at a level sufficient to maintain aggregate expenditure at FF'. This situation is obviously not viable in the long run, since there is a limit to foreign exchange reserves and international credit. Exchange depreciation will have to be resorted to eventually, since the government will probably regard this—unpalatable as it is—as a lesser evil than creating unemployment directly through deflation.

III

Much literature has been devoted to an analysis of the effects of a devaluation on the balance of payments. Earlier contributions by Joan Robinson, Fritz Machlup, and others concentrated on the magnitude of various elasticities of supply and demand for imports and exports as being the critical factors governing the extent to which the devaluation would be successful. Sidney Alexander proposed an alternative "absorption" approach, where the emphasis was on the impact of devaluation on income and total spending, the payments deficit being simply the difference between these two variables. In most contributions the existence of nontraded goods is ignored, except for a chapter in Meade's treatise and in an article by Pearce (1961).

The role of devaluation in the model used here is basically to alter the relative prices of traded and domestic goods in favor of the former, so as to increase production and reduce consumption until the two are equal. The price level of domestic goods, however, may be sensitive to the prices of traded goods and hence to the rate of exchange. Devaluation raises the cost of traded goods and hence reduces real wages to the extent that these enter workers' budgets. Strong unions could respond with successful claims for higher money wages, which would in turn raise the prices of domestic goods, which would induce further wage increases, and so on. Under these circumstances any given degree of depreciation of the exchange rate, which we shall call the nominal rate of devaluation, will be offset to some extent by a rise in the price level of domestic goods. Therefore, only the difference between the nominal rate of devaluation and the rate of increase of the domestic goods price level is what we shall call the *effective* rate of devaluation. The relationship between these three rates is set out in Figure 11.4. Along the horizontal axis we measure the nominal percentage change in the exchange rate. The curve OO′ shows the response of the domestic goods price level to a change of any given degree in the exchange rate, brought about by the mechanism described above and by the shift of demand to domestic goods as a result of the rise in the price of traded goods. The shape of the response function postulated is crucial to what follows. It is taken to slope upward at an increasing rate. By drawing a 45-degree line we can measure the effective rate of devaluation corresponding to any given nominal rate by the distance between the 45-degree line and the response curve OO′.

Social and political forces are the underlying factors behind the

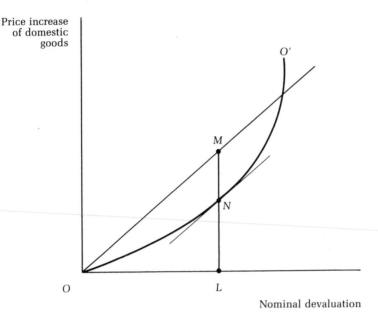

Figure 11.4

shape of the response function. The hypothesis is that the intensity of response by workers in pressing and obtaining money wage
claims rises more than proportionately to the challenge to their
living standards presented by any given degree of nominal
devaluation. The implication of the assumed shape of the response function is that there is a maximum feasible degree of effective devaluation, measured by the distance MN in Figure 11.4,
which is obtained when the nominal rate of devaluation is OL.
Larger nominal devaluations than OL are self-defeating, because
they result in lower rates of effective devaluation.[3]

As we have seen, the policy of maintaining full employment in
the presence of a structural imbalance between demand and sup-

[3] It would undoubtedly be desirable to build up such a functional relationship
from more precise specifications of money wage and price determination. As it
stands it is simply a crude attempt to formulate analytically the oft-repeated structuralist assertion that devaluation "won't work."

ply in each market results in a permanent trade deficit that must inevitably give rise to devaluation. When the devaluation is undertaken it is unlikely that the authorities can have any clear idea in advance of what the repercussion of money wages and the domestic-sector price level is going to be. If the repercussion is ignored, the nominal devaluation is quite likely to be too small in relation to the size of the balance of payments gap to be closed. On the other hand, if it is recognized that some reaction will occur the tendency will be to make the nominal devaluation very sizable, on the supposition that the effective rate is a monotonically increasing function of the nominal rate. With the shape of the response function assumed, however, too much may be as ineffective as too little, in terms of bringing about the correct relative price alignment between domestic and traded goods.

In addition to the relative price effect, however, devaluation also has an "absorption" effect, and in this case it is true that the larger the nominal devaluation the larger its impact on the trade deficit, if the money supply is held constant. The reason is that since the rise in the domestic-goods price level is an increasing function of the nominal rate of devaluation, so also is the general price level. Therefore, with money supply constant real expenditure must decline unless the velocity of circulation increases proportionately to the price level; this is highly unlikely. The trade deficit would be reduced, but at the price of both inflation and unemployment. With a constant money supply the unemployment will be greater the greater the degree of cost-push inflation induced by the devaluation. This phenomenon of higher inflation being correlated with higher unemployment has prompted Paul Streeten to observe that in Argentina normal economic laws seem to be reversed and the Phillips curve slopes upward.[4] If the government remains passive, unemployment and real income decline will spread through the multiplier process until the point R in Figure 11.3 is reached.

It might be asked why there is no expansion in the traded goods sector, under the twin stimuli of improved relative prices and

[4]See *Economic Journal*, 1969 p. 949.

greater availability of labor. This will happen in the long run but the critical factor is the speed at which this is likely to take place in comparison with the contractional process described above. Real income changes are generally much quicker acting than relative prices changes, particularly if there are institutional forces making for low factor mobility. It is likely that long before resource reallocation can bring about a full adjustment, pressure would have been created to end the depression by expansionary monetary and fiscal policy, at which point the story begins all over again. A succession of such cycles would produce the marked secular decline that has been observed in the internal and external purchasing power of several Latin American currencies. These episodes might however be combined with the more commonplace cause of inflation and exchange depreciation, which is merely excessive creation of money.

IV

The "structuralist" model described in the earlier sections has obvious implications for stabilization policy. In this final section we shall attempt to spell them out, and at the same time comment on why stabilization efforts based on the "monetarist" model might possibly do more harm than good.

In any situation for which the structuralist model is relevant the objective of policy should be to secure a readjustment of relative prices while at the same time maintaining a sufficient level of real expenditure to prevent unemployment from emerging in the domestic goods sector. As the readjustment of relative prices proceeds resources would be attracted to the traded goods sector, so that the level of total real expenditure needed to sustain employment in the domestic goods sector can be reduced, at a rate governed by the speed at which the economy can transform resources from the domestic to the traded goods sector. When the equilibrium level of relative price adjustment has been reached, and resource allocation is in conformity with it, total real expenditure can be brought down to a level that will sustain full employment without a trade deficit, since the structural imbalance that was creating the necessity of a trade deficit at full employment would have been removed.

The degree of reletive price adjustment required depends on the difference between the prevailing level and that which will secure equilibrium in the "real" part of the system. The latter will depend upon demand patterns, factor endowments, and technological conditions on the supply side. If one assumes that this required alteration of relative prices has been estimated, one is still faced with the problem of how to bring it about. As we have seen a nominal devaluation of just the required amount will not be sufficient, since the response of the domestic-goods price level has to be allowed for. Once the response function of Figure 11.4 is taken into account, the required effective devaluation can be measured between OO' and the 45-degree line, and the nominal devaluation necessary to bring this about read off the horizontal axis. All of this process of relative price adjustment should take place against a background of employment maintenance, by adjusting the money supply sufficiently to prevent the absolute price rises from having a deflationary effect. Adequate foreign exchange credits will also have to be supplied to cover the transition period to equilibrium.

The shift in relative prices brought about by an effective devaluation works to close the trade gap in two ways: it reduces the consumption of traded goods relative to domestic goods, and it shifts relative output levels of the two sectors in favor of traded goods. The production effect is likely to take much longer to work itself out, particularly if the various institutional rigidities that the structuralists mention actually do exist. The consumption effect, however, can be attained much more promptly; and assuming that the elasticity of substitution in consumption is not zero, any shift in relative prices taking place as a result of devaluation means that total real expenditure can be reduced to some extent while the demand for domestic goods is maintained at a constant level to prevent the creation of any unemployment. This means that the trade deficit can be reduced to some extent, even if output levels in the two sectors are constant in the short run. A sufficiently large shift in relative prices, if feasible, could wipe out the trade deficit altogether through the consumption effect alone. The relative price ratio required for this will be indicated by the slope of the indifference curve through Q in Figure 11.3. As time passes the production effect would start to work and hence create a tendency for a trade surplus. If the shift in relative prices required to close the deficit through the consumption effect alone is in excess of that required to bring about equilibrium when the production effect has worked itself out fully, the surplus will be permanent. Once the equilibrium production point is attained, however, overshooting could be prevented by appreciating the exchange rate or letting the price level of domestic goods increase by an appropriate injection of excess demand. The speed of transformation could plausibly be an increasing function of the magnitude of the relative price shift and so the overeffective devaluation policy could conceivably bring about the required adjustment in a shorter period of time and with no need for reserves to finance the transition.

We have also demonstrated that the limited or slow capacity to transform mentioned by the structuralists as a factor making devaluation inappropriate is not by itself a sufficient reason why a trade deficit cannot be closed by devaluation while maintaining full employment, since it ignores the effect of devaluation on the pattern of consumption. Devaluation will be less potent, however, the lower the elasticity of substitution in consumption between traded and domestic goods, and the closer the response function lies to the 45-degree line.

While it is obvious that in practice it will be extremely difficult to carry out the above "ideal" stabilization policy, it might nevertheless serve to provide a useful contrast to a strictly monetarist policy, in which the main features would be a large nominal devaluation to prevent expectations of a further devaluation and strict control of the money supply. Such a policy pays no explicit attention to the relative price effect of devaluation, and logically should even welcome cost-push effects on the price level so long as the money supply restrictions are adhered to, since this will enhance the deflationary impact of the program. Sufficiently drastic measures could clearly eliminate the trade deficit in a short time, but only at the price of unemployment. The resulting balance of payments situation could hardly be called an equilibrium one, if the widely accepted Nurkse definition of that term is used. Such attempts at "stabilization" have been the cause of much hostility to the I.M.F. in Latin America.

On the other hand it should not be denied that many instances of inflation could well be due to the conventional monetary reasons for which the orthodox proposals would give the right answer, provided the prices and wages in the expanded domestic goods sector are not inflexible at their higher levels and that labor is still sufficiently mobile.

The upshot of our discussion is that inflation and stabilization in contexts such as the Latin American one cannot always be viewed as financial phenomena, independent of the underlying real forces. Money supply, nominal exchange rates, and absolute price levels alone are not the heart of the matter: the relationship between the demand and supply for traded and domestic goods, the extent to which real disequilibria are translated into effective relative price signals, and the speed with which factors of production are allocated in response to them.

References

Amano, A. 1964. "Determinants of Comparative Costs: A Theoretical Approach." *Oxford Economic Papers* (November).

Arrow, K. 1968. "Optimal Capital Policy with Irreversible Investment." In *Value, Capital and Growth*, ed. J. N. Wolfe, Chicago: Adline.

Atkinson, A. B. 1969. "Import Strategy and Growth Under Conditions of Stagnant Export Earnings." *Oxford Economic Papers* (November).

Bacha, E. and Taylor, L. 1971. "Foreign Exchange Shadow Prices: A Critical Review of Current Theories." *Quarterly Journal of Economics* (May).

Baer, W. and Kerstenetzky, I. (eds.) 1964. *Inflation and Growth in Latin America*. New Haven: Yale University Press.

Balassa, B. and Schydlowsky, D. M. 1968. "Effective Tariffs, Domestic Cost of Foreign Exchange and the Equilibrium Exchange Rate." *Journal of Political Economy* (June).

Balogh, T. 1963. *Unequal Partners*. London: Basil Blackwell.

Bardhan, P. K. 1970. *Economic Growth, Development and Foreign Trade*. New York: Wiley.

Bhagwati, J. 1958. "Immiserizing Growth: A Geometrical Note." *Review of Economic Studies* (June).

——1966. "The Balance of Payments Difficulties of the Less Developed Countries." In *Measures for Trade Expansion of Developing Countries*, Japan Economic Research Center.

——and Ramaswami, V. K. 1963. "Domestic Distortions, Tariffs and the Theory of Optimum Subsidy." *Journal of Political Economy* (February).

——and Srinivasan, T. N. 1969. "Optimal Intervention to Achieve Noneconomic Objectives." *Review of Economic Studies* (January).

Bruno, M. 1963. *Interdependence, Resource Use and Structural Change in Israel*. Jerusalem: Bank of Israel.

221

Bruno, M. 1967. "The Optimal Selection of Export-Promoting and Import-Substituting Projects." In *Planning the External Sector*. New York: United Nations.

Cagan, P. 1956. "The Monetary Dynamics of Hyperinflation." In *Studies in the Quantity Theory of Money*, ed. M. Friedman. Chicago: University of Chicago Press.

Chenery, H. and Bruno, M. 1962. "Development Alternatives in an Open Economy: the Case of Israel." *Economic Journal* (March).

——and Strout, A. 1966. "Foreign Assistance and Economic Development." *American Economic Review* (September).

Corden, W. M. 1960. "The Geometric Representation of Policies to Attain Internal and External Balance." *Review of Economic Studies* (October).

——1969. "Effective Protective Rates in the General Equilibrium Model: A Geometric Note." *Oxford Economic Papers* (July).

——1971. "The Effects of Trade on the Rate of Growth." In *Trade, Balance of Payments and Growth*, eds. J. Bhagwati et al. Amsterdam: North Holland.

Diaz Alejandro, C. F. 1965. *Exchange Rate Devaluation in a Semi-Industrialized Country*. Cambridge, Mass.: M.I.T. Press.

——1970. *Essays on the Economic History of the Argentine Republic*. New Haven: Yale University Press.

Dixit, A. K. 1968. "Optimal Development in the Labour-Surplus Economy." *Review of Economic Studies* (January).

——1969. "Marketable Surplus and Dual Development." *Journal of Economic Theory* (August).

Dobb, M. H. 1960. *An Essay on Economic Growth and Planning*. London: Routledge and Kegan Paul.

Domar, E. D. 1957. *Essays in the Theory of Economic Growth*. London: Oxford University Press.

Dorfman, R., Samuelson, P. A., and Solow, R. M. 1958. *Linear Programming and Economic Analysis*. New York: McGraw-Hill.

Eckstein, O. 1957. "Investment Criteria for Economic Development and the Theory of Intertemporal Welfare Economics." *Quarterly Journal of Economics* (February).

Edgeworth, F. Y. 1894. "The Theory of International Values I." *Economic Journal* (March).

Erlich, A. 1950. "Preobrazhenski and the Economics of Soviet Industrialization." *Quarterly Journal of Economics* (February).

——1960. *The Soviet Industrialization Debate*. Cambridge, Mass.: Harvard University Press.

Fei, J. C. H. and Ranis, G. 1964. *Development of the Labor Surplus Economy*. Homewood, Ill.: Irwin.

Findlay, R. 1962. "Capital Theory and Developmental Planning." *Review of Economic Studies* (February).

——1966. "Optimal Investment Allocation between Consumer Goods and Capital Goods." *Economic Journal* (March).

——1970. "Factor Proportions and Comparative Advantage in the Long Run." *Journal of Political Economy* (February).

——1971a. "Comparative Advantage, "Effective Protection and the Domestic Resource Cost of Foreign Exchange." *Journal of International Economics* (May).

——1971b. "The Foreign Exchange Gap and Growth in Developing Economies." In *Trade, Balance of Payments and Growth*, eds. J. Bhagwati et al. Amsterdam: North Holland.

——and Grubert, H. 1959. "Factor Intensities, Technological Progress and the Terms of Trade." *Oxford Economic Papers* (February).

Galenson, W. and Leibenstein, H. 1955. "Investment Criteria, Productivity and Economic Development." *Quarterly Journal of Economics* (August).

Haberler, G. 1961. "Terms of Trade and Economic Development." In *Economic Development of Latin America*, ed. H. Ellis. New York: St. Martin's Press.

Hagen, E. E. 1958. "An Economic Justification of Protectionism." *Quarterly Journal of Economics* (November).

Hansen, B. 1967. *Long and Short Term Planning in Underdeveloped Countries*. Amsterdam: North Holland.

Hicks, J.R. 1953. "An Inaugural Lecture" *Oxford Economic Papers* (June).

Hirschmann, A. O. 1958. *The Strategy of Economic Development*, New Haven: Yale University Press.

Hornby, J. N. 1968. "Investment and Trade Policy in the Dual Economy." *Economic Journal* (March).

Johnson, H. G. 1955. "Economic Expansion and International Trade." *Manchester School* (May).

—— 1958. *International Trade and Economic Growth*. Cambridge: Harvard University Press.

——1959. "Economic Development and International Trade." *Nationalokonomisk Tidsskrift*. Reprinted as chapter 4 of Johnson 1962. *Money, Trade and Economic Growth*. Cambridge, Mass.: Harvard University Press.

——1966. "Factor Market Distortions and the Shape of the Transformation Curve." *Econometrica* (July).

Jones, R. 1956. "Factor Endowment and the Heckscher-Ohlin Model." *Review of Economic Studies* (October).

——1965. "The Structure of Simple General Equilibrium Models." *Journal of Political Economy* (December).

Jorgenson, D. W. 1961. "The Development of a Dual Economy." *Economic Journal* (June).

Kemp, M. 1969. *The Pure Theory of International Trade and Investment*. Englewood Cliffs, N.J.: Prentice-Hall.

Kenen, P. B. 1965. "Nature, Capital and Trade." *Journal of Political Economy* (October).

Kindleberger, C. P. 1956. *The Terms of Trade: A European Case Study*. New York: Wiley.

Komiya, R. 1967. "Non-traded Goods and the Pure Theory of International Trade." *International Economic Review* (June).

Kravis, I. B. 1970. "Trade as a Handmaiden of Growth: Similarities between the Nineteenth and Twentieth Centuries" *Economic Journal* (December).

Krueger, A. "Some Economic Costs of Exchange Control: The Turkish Case." *Journal of Political Economy* (October).

——1972. "Evaluating Restrictionist Trade Regimes: Theory and Measurement." *Journal of Political Economy* (February).

Lancaster, K. 1968. *Mathematical Economics*. New York: Macmillan.

Lary, H. B. 1968. *Imports of Manufactures from Less Developed Countries*. New York: Columbia University Press for the National Bureau of Economic Research.

Lefeber, L. 1971. "Trade and Minimum Wage Rates." In *Trade, Balance of Payments and Growth*, eds. J. Bhagwati et al. Amsterdam: North Holland.

Lerner, A. P. 1952. "Factor Prices and International Trade." *Economica* (February).

Lewis, S. and Guisinger, S. 1968. "Measuring Protection in a Developing Economy: The Case of Pakistan." *Journal of Political Economy* (December).

Lewis, W. A. 1954. "Economic Development with Unlimited Supplies of Labour." *Manchester School* (May).

—— 1955. *The Theory of Economic Growth*. London: George Allen and Unwin.

—— 1968. "Reflections on Unlimited Labour." Discussion Paper No. 5. Princeton: Development Research Project.

—— 1969. *Aspects of Tropical Trade 1883-1965*. Stockholm: Almiqvist and Wiksell.

Linder, S. B. 1967. *Trade and Trade Policy for Development*. New York: Praeger.

Lipsey, R. E. 1963. *Price and Quantity Trends in the Foreign Trade of the United States*. Princeton: Princeton University Press.

Little, I. M. D. and Mirrlees, J. M. 1969. *Manual of Industrial Project Analysis in Developing Countries*. OECD, Paris.

Mabro, J. 1967. "Optimal Investment Allocation between Consumer Goods and Capital Goods: A Comment." *Economic Journal* (September).

McKinnon, R. I. 1964. "Foreign Exchange Constraints in Economic Development and Efficient Aid Allocation." *Economic Journal* (June).

Mahalanobis, P. C. 1953. "Some Observations on the Process of Growth of National Income." *Sankhya* (September).

Marglin, S. 1967. "The Rate of Interest and the Value of Capital with Unlimited Supplies of Labor." *Essays on the Theory of Optimal Growth*, ed. K. L. Shell. Cambridge: M.I.T. Press.

Marshall, A. 1920. *Principles of Economics*. 8th ed. London: Macmillan.

Meier, G. M. 1968. *The International Economics of Development*. New York: Harper and Row.

Myrdal, G. 1956. *An International Economy*, New York: Harper and Row.

—— 1957. *Economic Theory and the Underdeveloped Regions*. London: Duckworth.

Nelson, R. 1970. "The Effective Exchange Rate: Employment and Growth in a Foreign Exchange–Constrained Economy." *Journal of Political Economy* (June).

Nurkse, R. 1953. *Problems of Capital Formation in Underdeveloped Countries*. Oxford.

——1959. *Patterns of Trade and Development*. Stockholm: Almqvist and Wiksell.

Olivera, J. H. G. 1964. "On Structural Inflation and Latin American Structuralism." *Oxford Economic Papers* (November).

Oniki, H. and Uzawa, H. 1965. "Patterns of Trade and Investment in a Dynamic Model of International Trade." *Review of Economic Studies* (January).

Pearce, I. F. 1961. "The Problem of the Balance of Payments." *International Economic Review* (January).

Raj, K. N. and Sen, A. K. 1961. "Alternative Patterns of Growth Under Conditions of Stagnant Export Earnings." *Oxford Economic Papers* (February).

Ramsey, F. 1928. "A Mathematical Theory of Savings." *Economic Journal* (December).

Robertson, D. H. 1915. *A Study of Industrial Fluctuation*. London: P. S. King and Son.

—— 1938. "The Future of International Trade." *Economic Journal* (March).

Robinson, J. 1970. "Capital Theory up to Date." *Canadian Journal of Economics* (May).

Robinson, R. 1956. "Factor Proportions and Comparative Advantage." *Quarterly Journal of Economics* (May).

Rosenstein-Rodan, P. 1943. "Problems of Industrialization of Eastern and South-Eastern Europe." *Economic Journal* (September).

Rostow, W. W. 1952. *The Process of Economic Growth*. New York: Norton.

Ruffin, R. 1969. "Tariffs, Intermediate Goods and Domestic Protection." *American Economic Review* (September).

Rybczynski, T. M. 1955. "Factor Endowments and Relative Commodity Prices." *Economica* (November).

Samuelson, P. A. 1949. "International Trade and Factor Price Equalization Once Again." *Economic Journal* (June).

—— (ed.) 1969. *International Economic Relations.* New York: St. Martin's Press.

Seers, D. 1962. "A Model of Comparative Rates of Growth in the World Economy." *Economic Journal* (March).

Sen, A. K. 1960. *Choice of Techniques.* London: Basil Blackwell.

—— 1966. "Peasants and Dualism with or without Surplus Labor." *Journal of Political Economy* (October).

Solow, R. M. 1956. "A Contribution to the Theory of Economic Growth." *Quarterly Journal of Economics* (February).

Stoleru, L. 1965. "An Optimal Policy for Economic Growth." *Econometrica* (April).

Swan, T. W. 1956. "Economic Growth and Capital Accumulation." *Economic Record* (November).

Takayama, A. 1964. "Economic Growth and International Trade." *Review of Economic Studies* (June).

United Nations, 1950. *The Economic Development of Latin America and Its Principal Problems.* New York.

Vanek, J. 1967. *Estimating Foreign Resource Needs for Economic Development.* New York: McGraw-Hill.

Vanek, J. 1968. *Maximal Economic Growth.* Ithaca: Cornell University Press.

Von Neumann, J. 1945–46. "A Model of General Economic Equilibrium." *Review of Economic Studies* (October).

Wan, H. Y. 1971. *Economic Growth.* New York: Harcourt Brace Jovanovich.

Wellisz, S. 1968. "Dual Economics, Disguised Unemployment and the Unlimited Supply of Labor." *Economica* (February).

Williamson, J. G. 1965. "Regional Inequality and the Process of National Development: A Description of the Pattern." *Economic Development and Cultural Change* (October).

Winter, S. 1967. "The Norm of a Closed Technology and the Straight-Down-the-Turnpike Theorem." *Review of Economic Studies* (January).

Index

NAMES

SUBJECTS